# Sublime Light on the Turin Shroud

Ludo Noens

# SUBLIME LIGHT ON THE TURIN SHROUD

The true origin of a controversial medieval relic

Aspekt Publishers

Illustrations:
- Front side of the Shroud of Turin:
Giuseppe Enrie photo, 1931.
- Transfiguration, 6th century.
St Catherine Monastery, Mount Sinai.

Translated and revised version of the Dutch 'Subliem Licht op de Lijkwade van Turijn', by Ludo Noens.
Aspekt Publishers, The Netherlands, 2015.

# SUBLIME LIGHT ON THE TURIN SHROUD

Original Dutch title: Subliem Licht op de Lijkwade van Turijn ©
2015 ASPEKT Publishers
© 2019 Aspekt Publishers
© Ludo Noens

Translation: © Ludo Noens

Aspekt Publishers | Amersfoortsestraat 27
3769 AD Soesterberg | The Netherlands
info@uitgeverijaspekt.nl | www.uitgeverijaspekt.nl

Cover design: Aspekt Graphics
Lay-out: Brigitte de Graaf & Thomas Wunderink

ISBN: 9789463385138
NUR: 680

Disclaimer – The author and the publisher have made every feasible effort to determine and acquire copyright permissions for material presented in this book. If any right-holders have been overlooked we kindly request them to apply to the publisher.

# Contents

**Introduction**    9

**I. The Turin Shroud**    13
Fire damage – Edessa – Constantinople – An awe-inspiring discovery – Shock – Science speaks – Radiation – The Maillard reaction – Painting – Stretched cloth – Photographic technique – Radiocarbon

**II. Powerful Works**    37
Outcast – Cynic – Source – Transfiguration – Roaming preacher – Pesher – Key figure – Son of God – Son of Man – Premonition – Suffering servant – Spiritual kingdom

**III. Death and Resurrection**    63
Empty tomb – Rapture – The glorified body – Touch – The sown body – Mysteries – Eleusis – Epopteia – The transcendent light – Ergot – Salutary dazzle

**IV. The Near-Death Experience**    91
Core Experiences – Susan Blackmore – Astral travellers – Stable model – Ketamine – Pim van Lommel – Ritual resurrection – Wisdom for the Perfects – Golden Flower

**V. The Holy Spirit**    111
The other Helper – Judeo-Christians – Baptism – Cathars – Immortal Garment – Secret Gospel of Mark – Lazarus – The Mysteries revisited – Baptism of Fire – Rebirth

## VI. The Light Body — 133
Body of Fire – Laser therapy – St. Elmo's fire – Human Batteries – Spontaneous human combustion – Biological plasma body – Metamorphosis – Bioluminescence – Anna Monaro – Fire Saints – Stigmata – Hysteria?

## VII. Kundalini — 159
Anomalies – Prana – Scientific research – Gopi Krishna – Evolution – Krishnamurti – The Infinite

## VIII. The Hesychasts — 177
Breathing technique – Symeon the New Theologian – Etheric light – Gregory Palamas – Patriarchal councils – Kingdom of God – Reanimating force

## IX. The Athos Shroud — 195
Vostitza – Identical replication – Seraphim of Sarov – Microwave radiation – Tachionic field – Jospice Imprint – Abba Sisoes – Icon

## References — 217

## Index — 229

With sincere thanks to my wife Kris H.

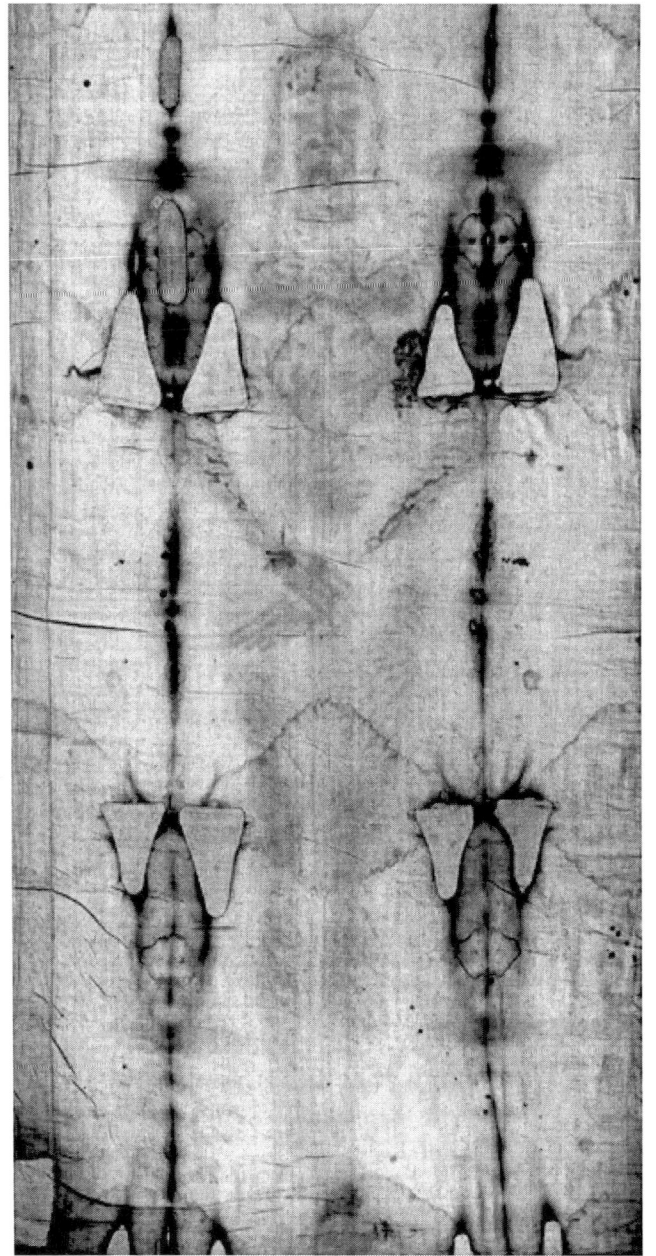

# INTRODUCTION

In April 1988, the Vatican agreed with the long-awaited radiocarbon dating of the controversial Turin Shroud, and ceded a 8 cm x 1 cm piece of the precious relic. Scientists were asked to determine the exact age of the supposed burial cloth of Jesus Christ. The experiment required an irreversible burning of the sample, which explains why it had taken so long before the Vatican authorities gave their final agreement; the newest techniques of the *Tandem Accelerator Mass Spectrometer* (TAMS) needed only a tiny part of the relic for the analysis.

In October of the same year, coordinator Dr Michael S. Tite of the British Museum presented the conclusion of the university labs of Oxford, Zurich and Tucson (Arizona) – the three labs had each received a tiny part of the cut-off strip – to the entire world press: the miraculous imprint of Jesus' resurrected body on the shroud dated to 1260-1390 CE...

Even if we accept that the Turin Shroud indeed is a cloth from the 13th or 14th century, this does not answer all questions raised before the carbon-14 dating. We will try to be reasonable, and trust the competence of the scientists involved. However, have they explained us unequivocally, unambiguously, and convincingly how the body imprint got on the Shroud?

Judging by the countless publications that have appeared in the scientific and the popular press since, it seems that nobody did manage so far.

At first sight, it was obvious that some poor dude had been flagellated and crucified in the Middle Ages, in the name of money (relic chasers) or religion (the mean Saracens). After all, things more repulsive happened during this calamitous 14th century, so colourfully described by the American historian Barbara Tuchman in her book *A Distant Mirror* (1978).

But how then did this subtle and durable imprint of a human body later get on the controversial textile? A myriad of hypotheses, yet not one satisfactory to explain this now somewhat desacralized enigma.

*'A miraculous phenomenon requires a miraculous explanation,'* argued Régine Pernoud. This French medieval historian examined at length the mysterious case of Joan of Arc. Her conclusion was: a divine intervention. Pernoud's Catholic religion will undoubtedly have guided her interpretation of the amazing exploits of the bold and visionary Maid of Orleans.

In this book, I have examined the case of the Turin Shroud with Pernoud's statement in mind: a preternatural phenomenon needs a preternatural explanation.

A preternatural phenomenon (Lat. *praeternaturalis,* 'said supernatural') is an unusual natural phenomenon that cannot adequately be explained with the actual scientific tools and knowledge.

Whether the absolute reality is rational or not, is not relevant here. The rational scientific method has undoubtedly proven its effectiveness in the analysis and interpretation of our day-to-day life experiences. In other words, at least our everyday macro-environment seems to be rational, logical and predictable, not unstable or chaotic.

With respect to the Turin Shroud, I decided first to follow all the rational tracks; and if I found no clue, I still had time to take another direction.

Rationality excludes prejudice, be it from a religious or a scientific viewpoint. The scientific method is (if not corrupted) an extremely rewarding research tool; it is a pity that ideological adherents of *scientism* have the tendency to absolutize this method in their scientific, naturalistic worldview.

Besides, the history of Science has taught us not to forget the evanescent character of most scientific theories.

Concerning the Turin linen, a physicist of the Los Alamos National Laboratory in New Mexico once declared, at the end of his tether:

*'We have done all possible tests, and none of them works. Apparently, we have only demonstrated that the Shroud does not exist. But it does exist.'*

So far the technological research.

Nevertheless, I think it is possible, within the limits of common sense, to rescue this awkward Shroud from its lonely marginality. To give it a place in history. To discover by comparison, deduction, and extrapolation its origin and the way how the contested image was imprinted on the cloth.

It is preposterous to argue against the scientific radiocarbon dating. The so called 'believers' recognize in the spectacular image instantly the 'stamp' of the Miracle Worker from Galilee, yet was it not this very Jesus who denied the unique character of his miracles?

Indeed,

*'Very truly, I tell you, the one who believes in me will also do the works that I do and, in fact, will do greater works than these, because I am going to the Father.'* (John 14:12)

The Turin Shroud was 'fabricated' in the 13th or 14th century. Even if something went wrong with the carbon-14 dating, at most a couple of centuries earlier.

Yet, not a smart swindler 'fabricated' the Shroud of Turin, but an 'enlightened' individual who had 'ears to hear' (Mark 4:23)…

# I

# THE TURIN SHROUD

The linen cloth, measuring 442 cm by 113 cm, is woven in flax, in a complex and rather rare herringbone twill. It shows, in delicate yellow sepia, the image of the front and the back of a naked, bearded, and long-haired man. The impression is as if a thirty- to forty-year-old man has lain for a short time between a long, double-folded sheet.

Judging by details on the cloth, one has the impression that the man died after violent maltreatment: traces of one hundred whiplashes, pierced wrists and feet, a stab wound in his right flank and something that looks like a thorn crown on the head. One discerns bloodstains and marks that seem to result from the torture.

Since 1694, and until recently, the linen has been conserved (rolled up) in a Silver Shrine of the Royal Chapel of Turin Cathedral in Italy. It is a unique piece, no other burial cloth has ever been found with such a perfect imprint of a human body. But then again, a body is seldom removed from its cloth before it can decompose...

The image on the Shroud of Turin (particularly because of the bloodstains) resembles strikingly the Jesus of the Gospels after he was taken from the Cross. Many people believe it is the original burial sheet in which Jesus the Nazorean was laid after his terrible suffering, some two thousand years ago.

The Shroud appeared for the first time in France during the Hundred Years' War. A French Knight, Geoffroi I de Charny, who died in battle in 1356, acquired the cloth in rather obscure circumstances. His widow had it displayed for a short time in the newly built little wooden church of Lirey, Champagne. The church authorities were initially sceptical; the stories on the origin of the cloth could not be verified.

Geoffroi had participated in a number of campaigns against the English, before he died in the battle of Poitiers. Moreover, in 1346 he had accompanied a Crusade against the Turks. Documents from that time praise his courage and religious devotion (He actually wrote a book on knightly virtues.) Even though he was acclaimed for his initiative to build a church dedicated to Mary on his territory, these documents do not mention his ownership of a miraculous shroud.

In 1389, Bishop Pierre d'Arcis of Troyes is the first to complain in a memorandum, on a fake *sudarium* of the Saviour. The rumour went that Geoffroi de Charny Jr. had it re-displayed to attract pilgrims. It was customary in those days to sell remembrance medallions of relics to pilgrims, undoubtedly a lucrative business. Five centuries later, in 1855, such a Shroud medallion was fished from muddy Seine waters; it had the coat of arms of Geoffroi Sr. and his wife Jeanne de Vergy.

Bishop Pierre d'Arcis, outraged, affirms that his predecessor Bishop Henri de Poitiers had already unmasked the fraudulent painter (Nevertheless, a letter of Henri dated May 28, 1356, only speaks in very flattering terms of the devote initiatives of Geoffroi.) d'Arcis also complains that the people explain both his and Henri de Poitier's wrath as mere jealousy for the unique and precious possession of de Charny.

King Charles VI wanted to confiscate the controversial relic, but without success. Clement VII, then anti-pope in Avignon, orders d'Arcis to silence. The disputed Church Father (family of Jeanne de Vergy's second husband Aymon de Genève) declares that Geoffroi I obtained the Shroud through his 'burning religious zeal'. He allows the linen to be displayed on special church holidays, on condition that it is shown only as a 'representation' of Jesus' tortured body (which corresponds more or less with Pope Francis' recent declarations thereon).

**Fire damage**

In 1449, Marguerite de Charny, daughter of Geoffroi II, tours for some time with the Shroud, and puts it on display in Chimay, near Liège (in nowadays Belgium). Cornelius Zantiflet, a suspicious Benedictine monk, writes that the Shroud is *'painted cleverly, hands, feet and flank covered with blood stains, as if the victim had only recently suffered the wounds and the stigmata'*.

In 1453, Marguerite offers the Shroud to Anne de Lusignan. Anne is the spouse of Louis I, Duke of Savoy, the house of the future Italian royal family.

Eighty years later, in 1532, the relic that hitherto had been conserved in the Sainte Chapelle of Chambéry, suffers severe fire damage.

Fortunately, the linen is fairly well conserved, despite the scorch spots caused by melting silver and the delineated contours of dried firewater. These fire and water traces are visible symmetrically on the cloth, as it lay folded in the shrine at the moment of disaster.

In 1534, the scorch spots are blurred rather clumsily by some patches of textile, sewn on the Shroud by Poor Clair Nuns (These patches were removed again in July 2002.) The nuns also fixed the Shroud onto a new linen cloth, known nowadays as the 'Dutch sheet'.

Even before the 1532 calamity, the Shroud had suffered from minor fire damage. Four holes in four L-shaped patterns were burned in the cloth, double folded at that time (the so called *poker holes*). According to some researchers, these holes are already visible on a representation of what could be the Turin Shroud, in a Hungarian manuscript dating from 1195.

In 1578, Duke Philibert of Savoy ordered the cloth to be brought to the John the Baptist Cathedral in Turin (It is said to spare the ailing Milanese Archbishop – and future saint – Carolus Borromeus a pilgrimage across the Alps.) In 1981 finally, after the death of his father Umberto II, Philibert's descendant, the mediagenic pretender to the throne Victor-Emmanuel of Savoy, donated the Shroud to the Holy See.

In April 1997, saved once more from a fire in the lush 17th century Chapel of priest-architect Guarino Guarini (The Chapel has been restored and was reopened in September 2018.), the Shroud was placed on a new spot in the Cathedral of Turin, behind the main altar. Today, the precious burial cloth is conserved in a heavily guarded relic shrine in the north side chapel of the Cathedral, next to the main altar, below the royal tribune. The Shroud has been placed on public display in spring 2010, and more recently in spring 2015.

**Edessa**

It was the British historian Ian Wilson who made the controversial Shroud of Turin world-famous. In his bestseller *The Turin Shroud* (1978), Wilson asserted that the relic could be traced back with reasonable accuracy, to the first century CE.

From the Syrian text *The Doctrine of Addai* from the 4th century, he concluded that after Jesus' Ascension, the Apostle Judas Thaddaeus (*Addai* in Syrian) took the miraculous burial cloth to the royal city of Edessa (nowadays Urfa, in southern Turkey). Apparently, Judas Thaddaeus, who was one of Jesus' brothers, hoped to cure King Abgar V of a disease (leprosy?), and enforce hereby his missionary work.

However, a closer reading of the original Syrian text would reveal that the name *Addai* does not refer to Judas Thaddaeus, but to the sceptical (Judas) Thomas, a forename that actually means 'twins' (John 20:24). The well-known apocryphal Gospel of Thomas is attributed to the latter.

Another legend, transmitted by the Greek theologian John of Damascus around 730, narrates how the court painter and archivist Hanan (or Ananias) travelled from Edessa to Jerusalem, hoping to meet the charismatic Nazorean and paint his portrait (the same story as how the *Doctrine of Addai* actually begins). Jesus, who realized that the artist failed to portray him because of the dazzling light that he radiated, solved the problem by covering himself with a *himation*, a large outer garment. By doing so, he imprinted the image of his body on the cloth.

After the death of the converted King Abgar V – who, according to the church historian Eusebius of Caesarea, had even corresponded with Jesus! – the town of Edessa returned to paganism. Ian Wilson thought that the few remaining faithful believers hid the cloth in a vault of the western city gate, where it remained buried for almost four centuries. Reconstruction of the city walls after a flood in 525 would eventually lead to its rediscovery.

## Constantinople

A 'face of Christ' on a rectangle of linen – known in the Eastern-Orthodox Church as the *Mandylion* – was venerated in Edessa as a miraculous relic for the next four centuries. This linen, Wilson says, was in fact the (Turin) Shroud shown 'doubled in four', revealing only the head of the Nazorean.

In 944, the Byzantine Emperor Romanus Lecapenus asked his general Johannes Curcuas to confiscate the relic. It was transported by Curcuas's intimidating forces to Constantinople, and afterwards described, in ambiguous terms, in a sermon by Gregory Referendarius, Archdeacon of the Hagia Sophia.

For Ian Wilson, it was thus higly probable that the *himation*, mentioned by John of Damascus, the Edessa Mandylion, and the Turin Shroud were the same relic.

Wilson pointed to the marked resemblance of the *Acheiropoietos* ((Medieval Greek: 'not made by human hands'), which is a type of icon representing Christ, and the long-haired and bearded head on the Turin Shroud. This type of portrait form became popular in the Byzantine Empire as early as the sixth century; it was thought to be inspired by the Edessa Mandylion. It is interesting to note here that the Eastern Orthodox Christians attribute supernatural properties to these icons.

The American historian Daniel S. Scavone drew the attention to the so called *epitaphioi threnoi*. These Weeping Robes were for the first time used in the $12^{th}$-$13^{th}$ century in the Greek liturgy during the Holy Week. They are graphical representations of the Man of Sorrows (sometimes life-sized) on canvas or frescoes.

Scavone and Wilson have argued that the Weeping Robes on which a suffering Christ figure is represented with a conspicuous aura and often with folded hands, is inspired by the man on the Turin linen.

In 1204, after the sack of the Byzantine capital by the troops of the Fourth Crusade, the 'Mandylion' disappeared. For Wilson it was the same cloth that the French Knight Robert de Clari, a year earlier, had seen there in the Church of St Mary of Blachernae, and that he had described as 'the shroud in which Our Lord had been wrapped'.

The American historian and lawyer Jack Markward has hypothesized that the linen was then put into security by the Bogomils or the Paulicians – Gnostic sects tolerated by the Orthodox Christians – and sent to the Cathars, their faith companions in the French Languedoc. The precious cloth was well-kept in the legendary Castle of Montségur, until the fortress was besieged and taken forty years later by the Catholic Inquisition. Markward suggested that this was the moment when the very religious Geoffroi de Charny received the precious relic as a royal gift.

In addition, Ian Wilson wondered whether there was a connection between the mysterious devotion that the Knights Templar showed for a long-haired and bearded head they called *Baphomet,* and Jesus' figure on the Shroud. For Wilson, it was possible that the Templars brought the linen to France in 1204 after the fall of Constantinople, and then guarded jealously and secretly this exclusive relic.

Nevertheless, even Ian Wilson assumed that a link with family members of Geoffroi de Charny from Byzantine Greece was a more plausible explanation for the appearance of the Shroud in France (details on this link in Chapter IX).

Christopher Knight and Robert Lomas have put forward a bold variation of the Knights Templar hypothesis. These two British Freemasons assert that the mysterious imprint on the Shroud is the image of Jacques de Molay. In 1314, in line with current practice in Ancient Rome, the Inquisition tortured in a mocking manner this last Grand Master of the renowned Order – who refused to accept the divinity of Christ – before burning him at the stake.

A clever theory that, for obvious reasons, historians hardly take seriously. Even the Edessa-link of

Ian Wilson, perhaps elaborated too speculatively, is accepted by relatively few academics.

**An awe-inspiring discovery**
The modern look at the Shroud started in 1898, when the Italian lawyer and amateur-photographer Secondo Pia took pictures of the linen, displayed to the public in Turin, that year. Much to his surprise, Pia discovered that the negative of his photograph (actually a positive image) gave a much clearer image of the imprint than that seen with the naked eye.

End of May 1931, twelve new, high-resolution photos were taken by professional photographer Giuseppe Enrie. The image of the tortured man on the cloth was visible at a higher definition, and more than ever a medieval forgery seemed excluded. Indeed, the 'negatives' appeared to be more lifelike than the allegedly painted original!

Around the turning of the 20$^{th}$ century, biologist Paul Vignon of the Institut Catholique in Paris had already performed revealing research concerning the linen. By covering plaster busts drenched in ammonia with tissue similar to the one of the Shroud, he managed to make images that strongly resembled the Turin image. Vignon noticed variations in the intensity of the imprinted image. His experiments showed that the darkest spots corresponded to places where the distance between the bust and the cloth was the shortest. The density of the projected image decreased as the distance between the cloth and the object increased. Vignon hypothesized that vaporized ammonia had left the imprint on the Shroud, ammonia that had been formed by the interaction of urea in the sweat of the tortured body and the myrrh and aloe with which the cloth was rubbed.

Vignon's *vaporographic* hypothesis has few adherents nowadays. In any case, analysis of a sample of the Shroud with a modern mass spectrometer at the University of Nebraska could find no trace of myrrh or aloe.

Vignon's observation of the varying density of the image, however, is still valid. Recent research has shown that this variation is not caused by a distinction in colour gradation but by a variation in density of the straw-yellow fibre tips on the linen surface.

## Shock

In the same year that Giuseppe Enrie made the sensational pictures of the Shroud, the case also fascinated Pierre Barbet, a deeply religious French surgeon. The grim experiments Dr Barbet performed on corpses seemed to indicate that the traditional representation of Jesus' pierced hands on paintings and sculptures could, literally and figuratively, no longer be held. Judging from the alleged traces of blood on the Shroud, it were the wrists, not the hand palms that had been pierced. Barbet identified the so called space of Destot as the spot where the nails had been driven into the wrists, causing, as stated by Barbet, the inward folding of the thumbs, resulting in the four-fingered hands on the Shroud.

Moreover, the feet appeared to have been nailed together, more exactly between the second and third metatarsal.

F.T. Zugibe, a pathologist from Columbia University, repeated Barbet's experiments, but came to a different conclusion. Zugibe argued that the wrist wound was the trace of the nail, as it protruded from the wrist, after it was first driven in the upper part of the palm, as written down in the Gospels and represented for centuries in the iconographic tradition. As to the invisible thumbs, Zugibe thought they were the mere consequence of a loose position of the hand.

Finally, he declared that the most probable cause of death had been *shock* (insufficient blood irrigation of vital organs), whereas Barbet had postulated a slow suffocation, resulting from the precarious hanging position on the cross.

Pierre Barbet affirmed that the man on the Shroud, whoever he had been, died as the result of a horrible crucifixion. Many details on the linen corresponded to the Gospels' description of the events that took place on Good Friday.

The head of the man, for instance, was mutilated with a monstrous fake crown, possibly a helmet of *Paliurus spina* or *Cordia myxa*, two Mediterranean bushes with razor-sharp thorns.

Appalling were the graphical traces of lashes (more than one hundred!) on the back of the body. These whip marks and other details became very visible in 1978, when the Shroud was photographed with ultraviolet light.

Two sadists in government service, standing each on one side of him, had apparently beaten up the unfortunate victim. The whip may well have been a *flagrum:* the leather strips of this Roman scourge ended in halter-shaped beads in bone or metal.

The face of the man on the Shroud seemed to Pierre Barbet also heavily disfigured: swollen nose, violated eyebrows, bruises and injuries on chin and cheek (cf. John 19:1-3). For Barbet, the result of Jesus' repeated falls on his painful way to Golgotha.

Finally, and perhaps the most mind-blowing, the French physician affirmed that there was a wound from a pointed weapon on the right side of the victim (between the fifth and sixth rib).

**Science speaks**

In the following paragraphs, I will sum up the opinion of a number of doctors and professors, at the risk that these titles may lose some of their glamour. Just to remind you, reader, that we have to do here with the eloquent disputes of eminent academics, not of uneducated pseudo-scientists.

In 1973, two Italian labs examined a small sample of linen and some torn fibres of the Shroud for traces of blood. Noteworthy, no actual blood substance was found, and it was determined that the image had a superficial appearance, i.e. it had not diffused into the tissue. The cellulose was modified in its structure only in the endings of its flaxen fibres, thereby contradicting Paul Vignon's urea theory.

The Belgian professor Gilbert Raes of the Textile Technology Institute in Ghent also examined the small piece of linen. His conclusion, as well as that of the Swiss pollen specialist Max Frei, was that the cloth had crossed Palestine and Turkey before arriving in 14$^{th}$ century France.

Raes had found fibres of a cotton variety *Gossypium herbaceum* in the cloth, for him a formal proof that the

Shroud originated in the Near East, whereas among the 49 pollen species that Prof. Frei discovered, a number were from plants only found in the Jordan valley.

One question, however, remained unanswered: why were there no pollen traces of the ubiquitous olive tree on the Shroud?

The most convincing proof of a 'natural' origin of the Shroud imprint was delivered in 1976 by the American physicists/Air Force Captains John P. Jackson and Eric J. Jumper.

Using high-tech instruments, they repeated Vignon's experiments. The observed density variations corresponded exactly with the distance between the body of a 'volunteer' and the folded cloth. They concluded that the undistorted print did not originate from direct contact, but through a vertical reaction at a short (less than 4 cm) distance.

In collaboration with Bill Mottern of Sandia Laboratories, John Jackson examined images of the Shroud with a VP8 Image Analyzer. This analog computer allowed to make an image in relief, after elimination of irrelevant background information.

The result surpassed the boldest expectations: on the screen of the VP8 appeared an actual 3D image of the famous face and body.

VP8 Image analysis also revealed an unnatural round thickening of the eyes. The Jesuit Prof. Francis Filas and Alan Whanger from Duke University later identified these as the traces of Roman coins. According to Jewish customs, a piece of money was laid on the eyes of the deceased.

Dr Whanger even distinguished the imprint of the Passion tools on the Shroud: spear, hammer, nails, sponge and dice. Even better, the Israeli botanist Avinoam Danin discovered the imprint of hundreds of flowers around the head, mostly from species typical of the Jerusalem area!

The imaginative interpretation of these 'Rorschach tests', as some called them, was met with a lot of scepticism. The Italian historian A. Lombatti, for instance, said he never heard of the Jewish burial ritual.

Nevertheless, one thing was certain. The man on the Shroud had his hair tied in a Sephardic ponytail on the back of his neck.

The Jackson and Jumper experiment was particularly important because of its three-dimensional reconstruction. Obtaining such an image is only possible when the intensity of the reflected light corresponds to the distance from the light source (for example in space photography). Normal photographs and images are not suitable for this type of analysis.

In any case, these extraordinary pictures made it clear that the imprint on the Shroud was something else than the work of a gifted painter.

**Radiation**

The American physicist Raymond R. Rogers thought initially that the delicate image was the result of a rapid ageing process of the fibre tips. Possible cause: a short-lived energetic radiation. Rogers called this hypothetical process *flash photolysis*. Eric Jumper stated that an intense laser light flash could explain such photolysis.

Images taken with UV fluorescence photography refuted burning by heat radiation, as the image of the body was not fluorescent, in contrast to the scorch spots.

For the French biophysicist (and priest) Jean Baptiste Rinaudo of the Faculté de Médecine in Montpellier, proton radiation could not be excluded. Whereas Thomas J. Phillips, a physicist at Harvard University, stated that neutron radiation was a possibility. It was even speculated that a flux of protons and neutrons had been liberated from disintegrated deuterium atoms in the body [sic], at the moment of its disappearance (the resurrection!).

What is surprising, and – as the French science historian Arnaud-Aaron Upinsky underlined – at least corresponds with the paradoxical ending of the four Gospels, is the fact that the Shroud does not show any signs of decomposition or 'removal of the body'. There are indeed no traces of loosened fibres or deformations of the tissue on places where the body must have lain.

So, do we have to believe that the body abruptly disappeared in the void?

Or were the sharply defined wound traces applied on the Shroud *afterwards*?

Lawyer/publicist Mark Antonacci even postulated the existence of a hypothetical 'cosmic wormhole' to explain the whole affair. Which led Raymond Rogers to state that such a dematerialization of a human body would generate more energy than the biggest hydrogen bomb ever!

The latest experiments with nuclear medicine equipment have convinced the physicist John Jackson (of the VP8 Image) of an organized emission and/or organized uptake of a so far unknown type of radiation. The image on the cloth would have been caused by the instantaneous desiccation and carbonisation of the fibre tips.

**The Maillard reaction**
In later years, Raymond Rogers dismissed his original radiation hypothesis, and shortly before he passed away in March 2005, he published a new theory. Rogers suggested that the faint image on the linen was the result of a naturally occurring chemical reaction. The so called Maillard reaction, an amino-carbonyl reaction, between reducing sugars from the bleached and starched (and not sufficiently rinsed) tissue and amino acid derivatives emanating from the corpse.

Required for this reaction were strict physiological and atmospheric conditions of the dead body and the environment respectively. Moreover, the cloth should have been removed from the dead body already within a couple of hours, before the appearance of cadaveric fluid (or during the alleged reanimation of the 'person concerned').

The gold-brown colouring of the fibres by a Maillard reaction, however, would need an elevated temperature (around 140 to 160°C) or else would take several days. Furthermore, the photorealistic character of the image on the Shroud remained unexplained.

Ray Rogers did not exclude that the Turin Shroud dated from the 1st century. A microchemical *vanillin* test on gradually disappearing *lignine* in the fibres of different parts of the linen, suggested to him that the tissue was at least 1300 years old.

Rogers's new conclusions were published in 2005 in *Thermochimica Acta*. Science journalist Philip Ball wrote admiringly of the paper in the prestigious journal *Nature*. Not surprisingly, Joe Nickell, the feared skeptic of the *Committee for Skeptical Inquiry* (formerly known as the *Committee for the Scientific Investigation of Claims of the Paranormal*) dismissed Rogers's paper as illogical nonsense!

## Painting

In October 1978, twenty-five American technicians travelled to Turin with their loads of equipment, financed by the *Shroud of Turin Research Project* (STURP). During the five days allotted to them, they generated a real archive of professional pictures of the Shroud.

Particularly the microphotographs revealed that the image was a paper-thin surface phenomenon. Fluorimetry showed that the 'blood stains' contained a percentage of iron, corresponding to that of real blood. Thus, it became clear that the 'blood' on the Shroud was indeed blood, not some red paint or whatsoever. It was even concluded that the blood group was of the rare AB type, even if the determining antibody reaction was weak.

The members of STURP found almost no pollen, whereas Max Frei, present once more, identified some 59 different pollen species on a selection of sticky tapes.

Twenty years later, Steven D. Schafersman of Texas University wrote that Frei had fooled himself. Or someone else had fooled him. For Schafersman it was not a coincidence that Frei had discovered exactly those pollen species that corroborated his conviction that the Shroud had originated in Palestine.

Shortly thereafter, another stubborn troublemaker stood up. Walter C. McCrone of the McCrone Research Institute in Chicago reported on his analysis of thirty-two pieces of tape that the STURP-team had used to collect thousands of fibres from different spots of the Shroud. Red ochre (coloured iron oxide) was visible on twenty of the strips that had been in contact with the body image covered with the alleged bloodstains. Furthermore, McCrone found traces of vermilion (mercury sulphate) on eleven pieces of tape that had been stripped from isolated bloodstains. Pieces of tape stripped from white parts of the Shroud did not have traces from either of these two pigments.

The initial conclusion by McCrone (deceased in 2002) was clear: the tissue of the Shroud had been painted twice. First with a dilution of red ochre and next with a dilution of vermilion to emphasize the 'blood stains'.

Later, McCrone started to doubt his own conclusion. Nevertheless, pathologist Prof. Dr Michael Baden agreed with him:

*'The blood stains on the linen are too beautifully defined to be true. Dead bodies do not leave such traces on grave cloths.'*

## Stretched cloth

For Isabel Piczek, the Hungarian expert in mural paintings, glass windows and mosaics, McCrone and Baden were inexperienced amateurs.

Piczek had performed painstaking experiments with live models in her own studio. She concluded that nobody could have painted such a negative image with shortened perspective as on the Turin Shroud. The presence of millions of pigment particles did not represent a problem for her: they were the careless traces of paint left by dozens of known and unknown copyists of the Shroud.

The image is continuous, Piczek said, yet it is not a continuous paint layer, and there are no sweeping tracks. And she repeated that the image had an extreme surface appearance.

As for the 'blood' visible on some spots of the linen, in the opinion of Dr Gilbert Lavoie, Dr John Heller, and the chemist prof. Alan Adler it could be genuine blood. Adler's research demonstrated the presence of porphyrin, bilirubin, albumin and other blood substances, whereas Dr Victor Tryon of Texas University even found traces of denatured human DNA.

The research results of medical doctor Lavoie further demonstrated that the imprint of the body and the bloodstains did not have a common origin. His experiments showed that semi-coagulated blood traces had been applied on the linen after it had draped the mutilated head and torso of the victim. Lavoie argued that the *image* (of Jesus) itself had been imprinted on the stretched, uncreased cloth.

Physicist John Jackson claimed that the Shroud had dropped down horizontally at the precise moment when the body had disappeared in a radiation flash!

Interesting to note that some specialists considered the analysis of the bloodstains as worthless, as the fierce 1532 fire in the Chambéry Chapel would have destroyed all possible protein traces by its excessive heat.

**Photographic technique**

In 1994, the South-African physician Nicholas Allen asserted that the 'photonegative' imprint on the Shroud could be explained by applying the principle of the *camera obscura*, already known by the ancient Greek philosopher Aristotle.

A handy medieval craftsman had exposed in full sunlight a white dyed sculpture of Christ in front of a dark room, in which a cloth, drenched in silver nitrate, was suspended. For four days, the smart guy let the reflected UV-light penetrate via a quartz lens into the room and on the double folded tissue. Later, he repeated the whole procedure for Christ's backside. Next, he washed the linen in an ammonia solution (or plain urine) to obtain the straw-yellow fixed double image.

The painted or real blood was applied afterwards, and it bleached, according to Dr Allen, the surface, explaining why there was no yellowing of the tissue *under* the bloodstains (in contrast to the opinion of other researchers who thought that the blood had been present on the cloth before the image was created).

Allen spoke of a medieval photographic technique that had been lost in time (The British journalists Lynn Picknett and Clive Prince have argued that it was the famous Leonardo da Vinci who applied this technique to immortalize himself!) The South-African doctor showed his test results, which were impressive at first sight, yet could not convince everyone.

Certainly not Barrie Schwortz, who listed a number of fundamental differences with the original Shroud. Schwortz, the official documenting photographer for the Shroud of Turin Research Project of 1978, pointed at the shadows on the fake shroud, caused by the position(s) of the unique light source (the sun). The Turin Shroud lacked all traces of shadow formation. In the opinion of Schwortz, motionless frontal illumination was also excluded. The unexposed parts of the linen, such as those around the protruded hands, appeared to professional photographer Barrie Schwortz, rather the result of a short, but hefty, general and vertical effect from within the body. Moreover, the Shroud missed the well-defined 'clear line' so characteristic of Dr Allen's image.

Ian Wilson, on the other hand, was impressed by Allen's theory. For him, this was the most convincing evidence hitherto of the 'photographic' quality of the image (not a painting) and of the possibility that the image was the result of a reflection (or emission) of light or another radiation source.

Was it possible that an unknown radiation source could have created a visible image on a linen cloth not previously treated with a light-sensitive substance?

**Radiocarbon**

As already mentioned in the introduction, in April 1988, the Vatican had provided a small strip of tissue for the long-awaited radiocarbon dating of the Shroud. The final conclusion of the laboratories of Oxford, Zurich and Tucson was presented in October to the assembled world press by coordinator Michael S. Tite: the Turin Shroud was a medieval forgery from the 14th century…

The Tucson result was 646 +/- 31 years BP (i.e. *Before Present* or before 1950), Oxford had measured 750

+/- 30 years BP and Zurich finally 676 +/- 24 years BP. This resulted in a mean age of 691 +/- 31 years BP.

With a confidence interval of 95%, the Turin Shroud was estimated to date from between the years 1260 and 1390.

So far the verdict of the advanced carbon-14 dating.

A storm of protest and accusations at the address of the specialists followed. An international group of scientists who defended the authenticity of the Shroud assembled in Rome. In the television program *L'odyssée de l'étrange* on TF1, the French mathematician Arnaud-Aaron Upinsky pointed to a number of irregularities in the radiocarbon dating procedure.

The original protocol, approved by a group of experts before the beginning of the tests, had consisted in the removal of samples from different parts of the linen. Moreover, initially seven laboratories were supposed to participate. Yet, on the initiative of Prof. Luigi Gionella, scientific advisor of Archbishop Ballestrero, it was decided to remove only a small strip from the edge of the cloth. The sample was cut in two, one piece again cut in three fragments, which were sent to the famous research laboratories.

For Upinsky there was a large variation between the results, particularly the ones generated in Oxford. Moreover, it was known that radiocarbon dating was not always reliable for the age determination of archaeological artefacts.

For some scientists, chemical contamination or insufficient control for the presence of microorganisms could have increased the C-14 level. Dr Leoncio Garza-Valdès mentioned a *bioplastic coating* on the linen surface: a bacterial and fungal layer had distorted the results, and was actually the cause of the image formation. Others accepted the results, yet feared that the carbon-14 was not distributed equally on the Shroud.

Perhaps the tested sample, removed very close to the sample that Raes had examined, was a piece that had been repaired in the Middle Ages?

Later, Ray Rogers showed that the cotton present in the sample – and a $14^{th}$ century gum paint layer on the flaxen fibres – was lacking completely on other parts of the cloth.

In their daring book *The Jesus-conspiracy*, the German writers H. Kersten and E.R. Gruber nearly accused Dr Michael Tite of pure fraud.

In addition, other, more conventional dating laboratories had expressed their concerns about the new TAMS techniques that had been used.

Remained also the radiation theory that allegedly explained the appearance of the image on the Shroud. Dr J-B. Rinaudo of the Nuclear Medicine Department of the Faculty of Medicine in Montpellier had proposed his (not rationally explained) hypothesis of proton emission. His experiment on a piece of linen from an Egyptian mummy from the $1^{st}$ century showed that such irradiation interfered with radiocarbon measurements. The protons (or neutrons) could have been captured by the atoms of the Shroud, and converted the C-13 in an undefined number of extra C-14 isotopes.

In short, the 'decisive' carbon-14 dating of 1988 was (and still is) dismissed by a significant group of experts who had collaborated intensively with the research of the Shroud. The scientific papers of – often religious – protesters can be found on the highly successful Shroud of Turin Website of Editor and Founder Barrie Schwortz.

Here the shoe pinches: how is it possible that radiocarbon results point to the 13$^{th}$ or 14$^{th}$ century, when the sum of so much previous research allows for only one conclusion?

We know of one historical figure that may have had the exceptional, adequate psychobiophysical properties to put his 'stamp' on the Turin Shroud. This Man lived in the 1$^{st}$ century.

But did these adequate psychobiophysical properties remain that exceptional during the following centuries?...

# II

# POWERFUL FORCES

The Turin Shroud has the imprint of a naked body that shows all the signs of the Christian *Man of Sorrows:* Jesus the Nazorean (Greek: *Nazoraios.* Probably not derived from the city of Nazareth, but from the Hebrew word *nazir:* 'he who has taken a vow' or 'he who withdrew'.) Charged for agitation, the Roman occupiers condemned this Galilean Jew to death. He was flagellated, capped with a thorn crown and nailed to a cross or a stake.

The original Gospels in Greek (Lk 23:53, Mk 15:46 and Mk 27:59) mention a fine linen cloth *(sindona)*. Jesus' body was 'wrapped' in this sindona after his death.

If the somewhat divergent Gospel of John, 'the Apostle who was loved by Jesus', was really written by him, then John was the only one of the four Evangelists who actually saw the empty grave. Although historical-critical research has strong doubts about John's genuine authorship, it is presumed that his rather late Gospel is partially based on earlier sources.

In Chapters 19 and 20 of the Gospel according to John, there is mention of a number of wrappings *(ton othonion)* and of a separate sweat cloth *(soudarion)* that was laid on Jesus' heavily mutilated head before he was actually buried. This alleged cloth is still conserved as a relic in the San Salvador Cathedral in Oviedo, North of Spain.

The image on the Turin Shroud seems to show Jesus tortured to death. If we forget for a moment the nature and spreading of the bloodstains, who else but this remarkable Jew from Galilee could have left his, hitherto unexplained, imprint on the Shroud?

But then again, what justifies our presumption that Jesus possessed the required, exceptional psychobiophysical properties to leave his image on the linen?

Let us start by having a closer look at Jesus' unique personality, claims, and actions.

In the Christian religion, Jesus is the Son of God, even God himself. Pope Francis is cautious in his judgement, yet for many Roman Catholics, the image on the Turin Shroud is the visible evidence of Jesus' resurrection from death. In other words, the evidence of a supernatural event.

The question here is not whether there exists a powerful Creator, but whether *only* a unique and planned historical intervention of this supposed Creator is needed to explain the teachings, miracle works, and 'resurrection' of Jesus.

The Evangelists describe the charismatic Galilean as someone who can calm the storms, walk on the water, and multiply bread and fishes. He heals the sick and feeble-minded, lets blind people see and the deaf hear, forces the paralysed to walk and even has the dead rise from their tombs.

In his comprehensive work *Jewish Antiquities*, the 1st century Jewish-Hellenistic historian Flavius Josephus describes in a short and controversial passage the 'signs' of Jesus as *paradoxa*: sensational, unheard, surprising, and provocative works.

The Judaic Babylonian Talmud from the 5th century dismisses these, in many aspects, exceptional feats. Not as fraud, but as misleading popular sorcery.

Jesus feels force *(dynamin)* flow from him when a woman in the crowd, who had been suffering from haemorrhages for twelve years, and according to evangelist Mark has spent her entire fortune on heartless physicians, touches the border of his garment:

'*Immediately her haemorrhage stopped; and she felt in her body that she was healed of her disease.*' (Mark 5:29)

The apocryphal *Actions of Pilate* identifies this woman as Berenice (Latin spelling: Veronica). This is the legendary Veronica (*vera eikoon:* true image) who will later, during Jesus' Calvary to the Cross, wipe his blood and sweat with her veil. And on this veil, his mutilated face will be imprinted miraculously.

Jesus also made the following bold claim:

'*I am the resurrection and the life. Those who believe in me, even though they die, will live, and everyone who lives and believes in me will never die.*' (John 11:25, 26)

Furthermore:

'*For truly I tell you, if you have faith the size of a mustard seed, you will say to this mountain, "Move from here to there," and it will move; and nothing will be impossible for you.*' (Matthew 17:20)

**Outcast**

Was this startling man the long-expected Messiah of the Jewish people? Was he the militant Ruler, descendant of King David, foretold by the prophets of the Old Testament?

Particularly under the hated Roman occupation, the title Messiah (Hebr. *Mashiach)* referred to the ideal political leader figure – anointed monarch and prophet – who needed to restore urgently Israel's sovereignty. Between 63 BCE and 70 CE, the Romans crucified countless messiah pretenders in the territory later called Palestine. The time was ripe for self-declared prophets and rebellion leaders.

Jesus was an Aramaic-speaking Jew. Many of his testimonies in the canonical Gospels refer to the Old Testament (actually to the *Tenach* or Hebrew Bible; more specifically to the Greek or the free translation into Aramaic). Particularly the apocalyptic or end-of-time literature, *en vogue* in those days, seems to have influenced Jesus and/or the Evangelists.

Nevertheless, his cryptic declarations, his personal language, and his self-assured doings were somewhat out of place in the Jewish society of that time. Skeptically inclined historical-critical researchers often explain the figure of Jesus of Galilee as a 'mere' faithful Jew among the other Jews. The Jewish religion historian Don Jaffé also thinks that the historical Jesus was, despite his miraculous healings, not really an outcast. Yet, the Gospels make it clear that his fellow Jews thought Jesus was an odd character.

*'Who are you?'* they asked him (John 8:25).

Jesus' uncommon behaviour frightened many. Some were irritated by his risky socio-religious deeds and by his puzzling arguments full of dark imagery. Others even thought he was possessed by a ghost or a demon.

It is interesting to note that Jesus himself was surprised by their confusion:

*'Why do you not understand what I tell you?'*

Moreover, what to think of this statement:

*'Where I am going, you cannot come (…) You are from below, I am from above; you are of this world, I am not of this world.'* (John 8:22, 23)

So it is hardly surprising the obstinate Swiss paleo-contact adherent Erich von Däniken has suspected Jesus to be (the son of) an extra-terrestrial astronaut!

**Cynic**

Up to the present day – as it was in Jesus' time – this elusive troublemaker continues to elicit fierce discussions.

Gerd Theissen, a Heidelberg scholar of the New Testament, and particularly the former priest John Dominic Crossan, have discerned in Jesus' remarkable words and deeds the influence of the Greek Cynics. The teachings of Antisthenes (440-366 BCE) knew a revival in the 1st century Roman Empire. Especially in Galilee, this philosophy was relatively successful.

The Cynics were a sort of travelling beggars/wise guys who wanted to shock the citizens by their haughty and offensive declarations. Diogenes of Sinope, a pariah, lived in a tub in the streets of Athens; he is the archetypal example of these ascetic philosophers. Holding a burning lantern, he was seeking provocatively for 'a human being' in the crowded Athens marketplace.

The story goes that when Alexander the Great asked him what was his greatest wish, Diogenes only demanded him to do a step aside. The mighty Macedonian King and world conqueror was actually standing in his sun! An insolent answer, typical for the profound contempt of the Cynics for social rules and worldly aspirations.

It is a fact that Jesus also showed this uncompromising critique, radical attitude, and disdain for the establishment and the conventional values, that were so typical for the Cynics. John Crossan maintained that Jesus was a socially motivated revolutionary with a Cynical tongue.

What Crossan and his historical-critical colleagues seem to neglect, however, is that other aspect of Jesus, omnipresent in the Gospels, i.e. the miracle worker and the conqueror of death.

## Quelle

In 1985, John Crossan and the radical American Bible Researchers of the so called *Jesus Seminar* examined the original Gospels, and the Bible texts that were added later, using well-defined authenticity criteria.

The earliest Christian community would have conserved the (hypothetical) Q-texts (Q from *Quelle* or source), being the original words of Jesus. Apparently, these Q-texts are the basis of the common passages found in the Gospels of Matthew and Luke (who also used the orally transmitted or written Gospel of Mark, considered to be the oldest).

Probably, the Q-texts contained the words to which the Gospel according to Thomas refers *('These are the secret words, which the Living Jesus spoke, and which Didymus Judas Thomas has written down.')* The hypothetical Q-texts, assembled from the Gospels, are indeed often concordant with this early-Gnostic Gospel of Thomas.

Burton Mack, professor emeritus at the School of Theology in Claremont, California, compiled his own version of the Q-text. Mack classified the words of Jesus from the so called synoptic, largely parallel Gospels of Mark, Luke, and Matthew, according to the gradually changing image Jesus' disciples had of him:

In Q1, the (Cynical) moralist is talking.

In the later Q2 texts, Jesus the philosopher explains himself through parables.

In the still later Q3, the Son of God addresses the people.

The original Cynical Jesus' community has been compared with the hippies of the sixties, the dissident stray children and 'spongers' of the then counterculture.

The American apologetic and religion philosopher Gary Habermas, however, represents a group of researchers who have dismissed this drastic text critique with several interesting arguments.

The general trend among the radical historical-critical Bible exegetes has been one to neglect the numerous and explicitly mentioned miracle works of Jesus.

Yet, there must have been a so called SQ *(sign quelle)* as well; the canonical Gospels of Mark and John, seem to go back to a chronological 'miracle catalogue'. This would mean that those 'inconvenient' miracles and signs *(semeia)* are not fantasies added in later times.

So, was Jesus just a wandering Cynic? Today, philosophical handbooks treat the Cynic Diogenes as a mere shameless phrasemonger. Then, what kind of person was this carpenter from Galilee, that he became the most discussed and honoured figure in human history? That presently more than one third of humanity worships him as God or as the Only Son of God?

In any case, he was neither a philosopher nor a scribe, as his shocked fellow citizens asked themselves:

*'How does this man have such learning, when he has never been taught?'* (John 7:15)

Then Jesus answered them:

*'My teachings are not mine, but of him who sent me.'*

The Father sent Jesus. But *'where is your Father?'* the Jews asked.

The Aramaic word *Abba* (Father) for God was not that unusual for pious Jews at that time, but it is questionable whether Jesus had the Jewish God *Yahweh* in mind. Did he not reply:

*'You know neither me nor my Father. If you knew me, you would know my Father also.'* (John 8:19)

What does it mean to be ONE with whom Jesus called his (and our) almighty Father?

Besides his evident predisposition to what is called today *channelling*, it is apparent from the Gospels that Jesus must have had exceptional 'powers' which could hardly be thought human.

Because they were of a supernatural nature? Or simply because most humans are no longer familiar with these powers?

**Transfiguration**

Almost two thousand years ago, three fishermen from Galilee followed the wandering preacher at his request. On a high mountain, according to the tradition Mount Tabor, east of Nazareth, the bewildered three men witnessed his metamorphosis:

*'And he was transfigured before them, and his face shone like the sun, and his clothes became dazzling white.'* (Matthew 17:2)

The figure of Jesus cannot be fully understood and explained without taking into account this disturbing incident.

Disturbing and absurd. No reasonable person has ever seen another person suddenly emit light.

But is that really so?

On reading the four canonical Gospels, one has to notice that Jesus repeatedly refers to his 'secret knowledge of the Kingdom of God', destined only for 'eyes that can see and ears that can hear'.

In Matthew 13:14, Jesus cites the prophet Isaiah from the Old Testament:

*'You will indeed listen, but never understand, and you will indeed look, but never perceive.'*

Thus, for ordinary people, he passed the knowledge in the form of parables, but to his close disciples Jesus showed the 'real thing':

*'To you it has been given to know the secrets of the kingdom of heaven, but to them it has not been given.'* (Matthew 13:11)

*'Truly I tell you, many prophets and righteous people longed to see what you see, but did not see it, and to hear what you hear, but did not hear it.'* (Matthew 13:17)

Now, for an average Christian, these words obviously refer to the visible presence of the Messiah Jesus, Son of God.

But is this all, or was there more to it?

Particularly the Gospels of Mark and John – the former written first, the latter last, and both with Gnostic undertones – can leave the reader quite frustrated. Ignoring – insofar as possible – the later theological interpretations, one has to conclude that Jesus never showed the back of his tongue. His statements were often obscure and paradoxical. Jesus preached, Jesus taught, Jesus spread the word, is written in the Gospel of Mark (ending in mid-sentence). Yet WHAT he actually declared is never clearly specified.

On the other hand, moral reprimands are not lacking at all in Matthew or Luke. But how are these admonitions, destined for the common people, related to the concealed 'holy secrets of the Kingdom of God'?...

Furthermore, all these words were written down in the Gospels at the earliest thirty years after they were spoken.

It cannot be denied: the biographical-religious reports in the four Gospels are full of contradictions. Often they consist of dubiously constructed passages and antedated notions. Text critics of the already mentioned *Jesus Seminar* have recently attempted, using consensus authenticity criteria, to eliminate the apologetic and theological plaster of the texts.

Based on the often incomprehensible and possibly rearranged keywords, a number of liberal or apostate exegetes have concluded that Jesus was an ordinary magician, a swindler or a hallucinating, conceited lunatic.

As for example the Flemish philosopher, theologian and psychopathologist Herman H. Somers, who in his book *Jesus the Messiah,* diagnosed the man from Galilee as ready for the lunatic asylum. In the opinion of Somers, Jesus was a mere *paraphrene* or vain psychotic.

**Roaming preacher**
All seems to indicate that the historical Jesus was a provocative, sometimes unreasonably demanding, certainly not all-knowing, yet definitively honest person. *With a peculiar psychobiophysical constitution.* Communication problems were inevitable.

Apparently, it already started when he was still living at home. According to the Gospel of John, his four brothers witnessed his remarkable 'works', yet in the light of his eccentric behaviour and obscure sayings, they thought he was losing his mind. So they sent him walking (John 7:3-7) and wanted to protect him against himself (Mark 3:21). Later, Jesus took his distance from his brothers – and even from his mother.

It is a fact that his psychic and his physical functions clearly deviated from those of his fellow men (more about this in the next chapters). Undoubtedly, Jesus himself was the first to be surprised of his unusual psychobiophysical talents, whether innate or acquired somewhere around his thirtieth birthday.

Having grown up in a religion in which metaphysics and ethics are strongly interwoven, it is quite possible that from the start he explained his 'problem' in the context of the Jewish theology. As a carpenter, he had not received a higher education, though he probably understood the Greek language fairly well, and could read the then liturgical Hebrew. And he was certainly aware of the religious disputes of his time!

It is possible that Jesus initially had contacts with the mystically oriented and communally living Essene brotherhood, which was clearly an inspiration for his nephew, the radical ascetic John the Baptist.

Anyway, Jesus was soon to go his own way.

**Pesher**

A Jewish way of text interpretation, particularly known from the New Testament and the Dead Sea Scrolls, is called *pesher*. It concerns a way of discussing and explaining passages of the Old Testament, and translating these to actual situations or events; a prophetic word that is relevant for the present, or that points to a fulfilment in the future.

Following the example of Jesus (Luke 4:21), the Apostles, Paul, and the Evangelists used a similar sort of exegesis in their conversion work.

Acts 17:2-3 describes the method:

*'And Paul went in, as was his custom, and on three Sabbath days argued with them* (the Jews in the synagogue) *from the scriptures explaining and proving that it was necessary for the Messiah to suffer and to rise from the dead, and saying, "This is the Messiah, Jesus whom I am proclaiming to you."'*

The least one can say of these (often wrongly cited, sometimes nonexistent) references, is that they need a lot of goodwill to see the connection. Jesus adapted his words and actions regularly to have them coincide with alleged prophecies from the Old Testament! Particularly when it concerned passages dealing with the Son of Man (Daniel 7) or with the Suffering Servant of the Lord (Isaiah 53 and Psalm 22).

A curious example is found in Luke 22:37-38. During the Last Supper, Jesus orders his disciples to buy *swords*:
*'For I tell you, the scripture must be fulfilled in me: "And he was counted among the lawless", and indeed what is written about me is being fulfilled.'*
*'They said, "Lord, look, here are two swords." He replied, "It is enough."'*

Historical-critical Bible research has also indicated Jesus' familiarity with the Jewish-Hellenistic Books of Wisdom. In the Book of Proverbs in the Old Testament, a father tells his son to walk the path of the law, virtue and wisdom. A personalized Sophia (a more or less female aspect of God) also has her say. Especially in the last, already fairly theologizing Gospel of John, we can read that Jesus identified himself with this personified Wisdom.

**Key figure**

It cannot be excluded that these references to the Old Testament were later reinterpretations of the Evangelists. Nevertheless, it is certain that Jesus was genuinely convinced of his task as Saviour. This special vocation was so obvious to him, that he asked the Jews in a wondering manner:

*'How come that you do not understand what I tell you?'*

It is also clear that he deduced his alleged vocation from his unusual psychobiophysical skills.

When John the Baptist sent two of his followers to ask Jesus:

*'Are you the Messiah or do we have to wait for another?'*
Jesus replied:
*'Go and tell John what you have seen and heard: the blind receive their sight, the lame walk, the lepers are cleansed, the deaf hear, the dead are raised, the poor have good news brought to them. And blessed is anyone who takes no offense at me.'* (Luke 7:22-23)
And:
*'(…) The works that I do in my Father's name testify to me.'* (John 10:25)
And further:
*'Believe me that I am in the Father and the Father is in me; but if you do not, then believe me because of the works themselves.'* (John 14:11)

Jesus' growing conviction that he was the Miracle Worker and Liberator announced by the prophet Isaiah (Isaiah 35:4-6) sometimes may have led to a self-overestimation and overconfident behavior. His superior intelligence and provocative conduct ultimately resulted in a clash with the Jewish and Roman authorities.

Surely, 'the Messiah' (for the Jews a national-political liberation figure) had no high esteem for the worldly wisdoms and social conventions! Isn't it strange that up to the present day, the most reactionary and religious institutes continue to thrive in the name of this perfect example of the subversive non-conformist? One can indeed ask oneself how many of the hundreds of millions so-called Christians have ever read the four canonical Gospels all the way through!

Jesus showed more consideration for public women and the social underdogs than for the 'blind guides' and the 'well-acquainted with the law'. And words such as these were sharper than the mockery of the British satirist Jonathan Swift:

*'I praise you Father, Master of heaven and earth, because you have hidden these things from the wise and clever, and showed them to the little ones.'* (Lk 10:21)

Moreover, Jesus advised in all seriousness to abandon house and family, and certainly not to work for a living. He used to eat at tables of strangers and had no *'place upon which to lay his head'*.

And for those who envied him:

*'The twelve were with him, as well as some women who had been cured of evil spirits and infirmities: Mary, called Magdalene, from whom seven demons had gone out, and Joanna, the wife of Herod's steward Chuza, and Susanna, and many others, who provided for them out of their resources.'* (Luke 8:1-3)

Jesus even recommended to leave the burying of the dead to 'the dead' (Matthew 8:22), though on the authority of the *Jewish Encyclopedia* this text should be read as: *'Let the village people bury their dead.'*

Anyhow, in Luke 12:22-33 his message is clear:

*'Do not worry about your life, what you will eat, or about your body, what you will wear. For life is more than food, and the body more than clothing. Consider the ravens: they neither sow nor reap, they have neither storehouse nor barn, and yet God feeds them. Of how much more value are you than the birds! And can any of you by worrying add a single hour to your span of life? If then you are not able to do so small a thing as that, why do you worry about the rest? (...) And do*

*not keep striving for what you are to eat and what you are to drink, and do not keep worrying (...) Sell your possessions, and give alms (...)'*

And also the following is true: seldom had a man such a courage and moral integrity to stand up against hypocrisy and injustice, yet he was a fine-tuned person filled with compassion and understanding.

By the way, the Evangelists did their best to blame Jesus' martyrdom on the Jews, and to put the Romans out of the wind. For obvious reasons: the missionary work of the Hellenistic-oriented members of the Nazorean sect (as the first Christians were called) focused gradually on non-Jews, as success in their homeland was only minimal (as can be read in Matthew 10:5, and this despite Jesus' interdiction!). It was important for them not to offend openly the brutal occupant power.

In a letter of Paul to the Romans (Romans 13), the zealous Apostle to the Gentiles even openly praises the by God appointed (Roman) authorities. Which cannot be said of the Judeo-Christian John in his New Testament *Revelations:* he more or less insults the Roman occupant for being the dirt in the streets!

As for the blatant cursing of the Jews in the first letter of Paul to the Thessalonians (2:14-16, a license to later antisemitism), for some Bible scholars it is probable that this text was only added later.

Needless to say that not the Jewish people, but a number of high priests and scribes, appointed by the Roman authorities, preferred to get rid of the Jewish troublemaker Jesus. This uneducated, yet well-informed Galilean miracle worker – who spoke out loud of his personal contact with his omnipresent Father – had become a serious problem for the powerful, unpopular temple authorities.

**Son of God**
*'Then the righteous will shine like the sun in the Kingdom of their Father. Whoever has ears, let them hear,'* Jesus says.

There is little doubt that the institutionalized Christianity, even today, gives a wrong interpretation of the impressive signs, sayings and parables of this mysterious man. Much the same as did Jesus' early disciples, who repeatedly displeased him with their wrong conclusions, confusion and misunderstanding.

The letters of Paul testify of the occasional shameless quarrelling of these disciples about the true message of Jesus. Some apocryphal Gospels, mystic schools and later so-called heretic movements may have had a more correct understanding of his words. Undoubtedly, a number of them actually followed Jesus' original instructions.

The common Christian may not be aware of this, yet the doctors of the Church recognize it: Jesus has never declared that he was the Son of God in a genealogical sense. Or that he was God. In the Judaism of those days, 'Son of God' was a current honorary name used for a wise and just man.

In Psalms 2:7, Yahweh declares to King David, appointed by him:
*'You are my Son. Today I have become your Father.'* (cf. Mark 1:11: *'You are my Son, the Beloved; with you I am well pleased.'*)

The doctrine of God's only Son and the later Holy Trinity actually developed, among others, from the emanation philosophy of Philo, a Hellenistic diaspora Jew from the Egyptian port city Alexandria. Philo was a prosperous merchant, contemporary to Jesus, who wanted to reconcile Plato's theory of Forms (or Ideas) with the Creation story from the Book of Genesis.

The concept of *Logos*, i.e. the Word or the Reason behind al moving and changing things, was first introduced by the Ionian philosopher Heraclitus of Ephesus ($5^{th}$ century BCE), famous for his insistence on ever-present change as the fundamental essence of the universe.

The Logos, as the creative emanation of the Absolute God, the Firstborn son of God, the Image of God from which emanated the primordial Light, incarnated, according to John 1:1 and Paul, in the human being Jesus (as asserted by Philo also in the man Moses). Thus, the Galilean was assimilated with the Logos, and considered a part of the Godly nature.

This Christian doctrine, developed by the Hellenistic Jews and converts, readily identified the figure of a Logos-Jesus as the liberating Messiah (or Anointed) announced by the Jewish prophets. Through its Greek translation *Christos*, the initially, politically coloured Jewish title *Mashiach* acquired very quickly the more universal connotation of spiritual Redeemer.

Furthermore, the disputed letter of Paul to the Hebrews and the equally disputed letters of Peter and Judah, show the unmistakable influence of Philo's teachings on the invisible heavenly hierarchies: angels, authorities, powers and forces.

Besides, the same Philo of Alexandria, very popular among the early Church Fathers, exerted a major influence on the later refinements of the Christian theology.

**Son of Man**

It is difficult to say what Jesus the Nazorean would have thought of all this. The Evangelists tell us that he called himself the Light of the world, the Messianic 'Son of (a) Man' in which the Father is glorified. (Mark 13:26)

But Jesus may have referred to himself as *bar nasha* (a neutral Aramaic expression: the son of man, the man, someone, or I). In the Book of Ezekiel, this Old Testament prophet is also often addressed by Yahweh with the word 'son of man'.

The Messianic Son of Man is first mentioned in Daniel 7:13-14:

*'As I watched in the night visions, I saw one like a human being coming with the clouds of heaven. And he came to the Ancient One and was presented before him. To him was given dominion and glory and kingship, that all peoples, nations and languages should serve him. His dominion is an everlasting dominion that shall not pass away, and his kingship is one that shall never be destroyed.'*

In the *Book of Parables,* part of the Jewish apocryphal Book of Enoch (2nd century BCE, originally written in Aramaic), the author, who speaks as the antediluvian patriarch Enoch, identifies himself as the heavenly Messiah. Genesis 5:24 mentions briefly his mysterious 'disappearance':

*'Enoch walked with God; then he was no more, because God took him.'*

Besides of being called the Son of Man, in this Book of Enoch the alleged patriarch also is called the Just and the Chosen.

*'And it happened that my spirit was lifted up in the sky,'* pseudo-Enoch writes in Chapter 70, *'and I saw the holy sons of God. They stepped over flames of fire. Their cloths were white, and their faces shone like snow.'*

The Slavic Book 2 of Enoch (date uncertain, origin Greek or Hebrew), describes the actual metamorphosis of the Chosen Enoch into the shining archangel Metatron, God's universal governor.

In the later Book 3 of Enoch, this Metatron is even called 'the smaller Yahweh' or 'the lesser Yahweh'.

It is possible that Jesus identified himself, for specific reasons, with this Enoch/Son of Man/Metatron.

A Letter of Judah (verse 14) confirms that at least Book 1 of Enoch, discovered in Ethiopia, was known by Jesus' disciples.

Moreover, in his report of the Transfiguration, Evangelist Luke even uses the Enochian title 'my Chosen' (Luke 9):

*'And while he* (Jesus) *was praying, the appearance of his face changed, and his clothes became dazzling white (…) Then from the cloud came a voice that said, "This is my Son, my Chosen; listen to him!"'*

Christian Bible scholars agree that during the Roman occupation of the Palestinian region, the Jews identified the Son of Man from the Book of Daniel with the awaited Messiah, the Saviour of Israel. In the Gospels, Jesus is often alluded to as 'the Son of Man who has to be glorified' and 'the Son of Man who ascends or is lifted to heaven', which makes him equal to the Messiah.

*'Who do the crowds say that I am?'* a curious Jesus asks his disciples (Luke 9:18). They tell him that the people think he is one of the ancient prophets, because of the many miracles he has performed.

*'But who do you say that I am?'* Jesus asks Peter. And Peter answers *'The Messiah of God'* (the anointed Messiah, liberator of the Roman yoke).

If Jesus – encouraged by his disciples – really attributed himself the title 'King of the Jews', it is reasonable to accept that this was a somewhat overconfident misinterpretation of a person gifted with exceptional psychobiophysical abilities.

Either Jesus was afraid of the dangerous political connotation of the title, or he did not really take it seriously.

Anyway:

*'He sternly ordered and commanded them not to tell anyone.'*

## Premonition

*'Indeed, the days will come upon you,'* Jesus predicts shortly before he is captured (around the year 33 of the Christian era), *'when your enemies will set up ramparts around you and surround you, and hem you in on every side. They will crush you to the ground, you and your children within you, and they will not leave within you one stone upon another; because you did not recognize the time of your visitation from God.'*

The prophecy of Jesus regarding the catastrophic fall of Jerusalem in 70 CE and the traumatizing destruction of the Temple by the Romans (Mark 13 and Luke 19:43-

44) is assumed even by many Christian Bible scholars to have been written after the facts. Nevertheless, taking into account his psychobiophysical irregularities, and not discarding too hastily his paranormal abilities/works, the hypothesis that Jesus also had premonitory gifts is very plausible (In *Jewish Antiquities* of Flavius Josephus, he writes that the Essenes of those days were very talented in predicting the future as well).

This emotionally charged precognition must have tormented Jesus seriously. It is possible that the destruction prophecy in Daniel 9 and the prediction of the coming and thwarting of the Messiah may have reinforced his supposed vocation.

Let us compare Jesus' prophecy with an incident reported by W.H.C. Tenhaeff in his book *Oorlogsvoorspellingen* ('Predictions of War'), in which the Dutch parapsychologist discussed the link between neurosis and psychic talents, as well as the connection that native cultures make between a 'lightheaded' individual and 'God's chosen one'. Tenhaeff argued that persons with particular mental problems are proficient in making remarkable predictions.

Further, he maintained that general predictions by clairvoyants are often, if not always, related to personal or third-person experiences of the future. In the latter case, the clairvoyant would be able to telepathically pick up other persons' future observations (as in the case of the clairvoyant Jesus, who died – or at least 'disappeared' – a long time before the destruction of the Temple). For Tenhaeff, it invariably concerns heavy-laden, emotionally charged events.

As the German philosophers Leibniz and Schopenhauer, and the French parapsychologist Eugène Osty before him, Tenhaeff accepted the working hypothesis of a *Memory of the Future* to explain the countless cases of accurate precognition.

As an example he told the – remarkable in the context of our thesis – story of a certain Mrs M. Tenhaeff had known this woman for more than forty years and had full confidence in her.

In August 1939, Mr X, a business relation of her husband had ordered a large shipment of flour in the US. Her husband was waiting for a signature of this Mr X to store the freight in his warehouse in the *Scheepsmakershaven* of Rotterdam. But suddenly, Mr X retired from the business. '*He said that he was chosen and no longer allowed to handle earthly affairs.*' [sic!]

In the meantime it had become clear that Mr X had serious psychic problems. A meeting was arranged at his house, meeting were Mrs M. was present.

She told:

'*The wife of Mr X, more or less upset, tried to convince him to sign the papers. I told him that someday he might be grateful to my husband for having given himself so much trouble. My words were not received well. "No", he replied, standing up, "we shall turn around the case. Once, your husband will be grateful that I have refused to sign, because his office and storehouse are on fire. The whole of the* Bierhaven *is burning, as well as the* Schiedamse Dijk. *My business is burning; the whole of Rotterdam is on fire.*"

Next, he turned around, walked away, both his arms stretched in front of him, saying:

*"I am going to the Glory."* [sic again!]
*'(…) A couple of months later, Mr X was admitted to a psychiatric hospital, where he died in August 1940 (…) On May 14<sup>th</sup> 1940 an important part of Rotterdam (including the* Bierhaven, *the* Scheepsmakershaven *and the* Schiedamse Dijk) *was destroyed by fire. My husband – deceased in December 1943 – told me that he was glad that Mr X's flour cargo had not been stored in his warehouse, because it would have entailed a considerable financial loss for him…'*

## Suffering Servant

More than with the glorious Son of Man, Jesus identified himself with the Suffering Servant of the Lord from Isaiah 53 (actually Deutero-Isaiah; the author(s) of the Chapters 40-66 are not known by name).

*'(…) He was despised and rejected by others; a man of suffering and acquainted with infirmity (…) But he was wounded for our transgressions, crushed for our iniquities (…) He was oppressed, and he was afflicted, yet he did not open his mouth; like a lamb that is led to the slaughter, and like a sheep that before its shearers is silent, so he did not open his mouth (…)'* etc.

For the Jews, this Suffering Servant was a personification of Israel: the chosen, yet tried Jewish people (Isaiah 41:8-9). Jesus, however, gave this passage from the Hebrew Bible a self-referring prophetic reference.

As we can read in the Gospels, he anticipated his own suffering, martyrdom and resurrection! A fate that he could not comprehend and could only have meaning by coupling Daniel's victorious Messiah to the pseudo-prophecy of Isaiah.

> *'The Son of Man must undergo great suffering, and be rejected by the elders, chief priests and scribes, and be killed, and on the third day be raised.'* (Luke 9:22)

This notion of a Suffering Messiah was an absurdity for his disciples, as it still is now for the Jews. They were shocked:

> *'But they did not understand this saying; its meaning was concealed from them, so that they could not perceive it. And they were afraid to ask him about this saying.'* (Luke 9:45)

Jesus' ineluctable destiny is also mentioned explicitly in Lucas's version of Jesus' transfiguration on Mount Tabor:

> *'And while he was praying, the appearance of his face changed, and his clothes became dazzling white. Suddenly they saw two men, Moses and Elijah, talking to him. They appeared in glory, and were speaking of his departure, which he was about to accomplish at Jerusalem...'* (Luke 9:29-31)

## Spiritual Kingdom

After his shameful execution, it was clear to the Jews that Jesus could not have been the eagerly awaited Founder of a theocratically ruled Israel (the traditional 'Kingdom of God'). Yet the disciples remembered their mysterious, authoritative and untouchable *Rabboni*, a charismatic moralist who unmistakably had performed 'miracles'.

*Miracles that continued to happen even after his death.*

It were amazing phenomena, 'supernatural' enough to justify a rereading of the *Tenach* or Hebrew Bible. For eyewitnesses it was clear that Jesus, even though executed, had been someone with a mission from heaven. God's Kingdom and the title King of the Jews – words that the historical Jesus may never have used – referred to the Restored Israel that was to come very soon. A hope that Jesus' disciples wanted to justify in the writings they left.

This initial discrete rereading/reformulation by Law-abiding Jews, was later re-edited by Hellenistic-oriented authors, using artificial literary processes. And in a relatively short period of time, a new story, not too coherent and quite mythical, but appealing to more and more non-Jews, was written: the 'orthodox' Christian theology.

The Christian theology is a spiritualized and universalized adaptation of the practically oriented Old-Jewish theology of the Covenant (which, after the destruction of the Jewish Temple by the Romans in 70 CE, was only perpetuated by the Pharisaic school in the rabbinic Judaism of the Talmud, complementing the Torah with orally transmitted laws).

The radically different, and even today still evolving, Christian image of God was an attempt of a small circle of orthodox Jews to give an interpretation of the 'unbelievable' words and deeds of the historical Jesus that they had witnessed personally, and to give them significance and a reason of existence…

# III

# DEATH AND RESURRECTION

Almost two thousand years ago, Jesus the Nazorean, enigmatic Jewish wandering preacher, died on the cross in Jerusalem. His subversive speeches had become too much for the Roman and Jewish authorities. As the Sabbath was imminent, Jesus' heavily mutilated body was buried, for the time being, in the family tomb of his wealthy sympathizer Joseph of Arimathea.

According to the New Testament, Jesus resurrected on the second or the third day. Some five weeks later, he ascended physically to heaven on the Mount of Olives.

Jesus, we are told, was physically dead. And a little while later, he (or his 'heavenly Father') brought his dead body in a glorified state back to life. It is believed by many Christian scientists that during the initial stage of the resurrection, Jesus left the imprint of his body on the Turin Shroud.

In this chapter, we will elaborate on the how and why of that resurrection process.

First we will see what Paul, the Apostle of the Gentiles, has to say about this. Paul's *'why'* of Jesus' resurrection is the religious core of the actual Christian theology. Paul's *'how'* of the resurrection concords surprisingly well with meta-physical notions from other cultures and worldviews.

Paul was a Hellenized Jew who was strongly influenced by the Greek ideas of the dual nature of man: body and spirit (or soul). As maintained by Paul, Jesus' apparitions after his death were evidence that the soul of a faithful Christian survived his bodily death. When Christ would come at the End of Times (expected, in the first century, to be very soon) the faithful would also rise physically.

'Death is the punishment for sin', the disobedient first human couple was told. In the alternative theology of Paul, Judaic peace offerings and sincere repentance did no longer suffice to ensure the salvation of the sinner. The sinner had to accept that Jesus Christ, the Son of God, had sacrificed His temporary bodily form for his personal redemption. By doing so, the convert would instantly receive as a grace, or free gift, God's holy spirit, promise of the eternal life.

Since the time of the prophets (5th century BCE), some Old Testament Jews believed in the physical resurrection of the dead (Isaiah 26:19). This idea, coupled to Messianic expectations, was well established in the 2nd century BCE (Daniel 12:2-3).

In the New Testament it is written that the Pharisees defended the resurrection philosophy; the aristocratic but equally pious Sadducees in contrast, did not believe in a resurrection, nor in angels or demons for that matter.

Paul also believed in the resurrection of the dead body; in Philippians 3:5 he declares explicitly to have been a faultless Pharisee.

The New Testament does not mention the Essenes, who congregated in communal life. But other texts mention that this ascetic and mystically oriented Jewish sect also believed in an autonomous soul, as well as in the resurrection.

From the Gospels we know that the Pharisees were a separate school of scribes, applying the Mosaic laws (be it less literally than the Saducean priests), who strongly advocated ritual purity. Jesus, in many ways remarkably tolerant, was often in conflict with the Pharisees.

In some passages, Jesus also speaks about a general resurrection (although it can be questioned whether these passages are authentic). Anyway, the Pharisees had never heard someone predicting his personal resurrection, immediately after his death: this was the truly revolutionary claim of Jesus.

The Gospels repeatedly mention that even Jesus' disciples did not take him seriously on this matter. The humiliating martyrdom of their master caused indecisiveness and despair. Also for the Apostles, it was unthinkable that the Messiah would die on the cross (according to Deuteronomy 21:23 the most disgraceful death possible). And the empty tomb on Passover Sunday initially rendered their confusion even greater.

Fifty days later, a memorable thing happened in an upper room of a house in Jerusalem... When the holy spirit descended on the Apostles, things became clear in their head, both literally and figuratively speaking.

**Empty tomb**
Today we live the heyday of rationalism, science, and technology, with little room left for divine interventions and miracles. With the exception of a few adherents of the so called *Jesus Myth*, most liberal Christians do accept the historical existence of Jesus. However, they consider his physical resurrection a misunderstanding of the early Christians, or a symbol.

Protestant theologians, such as Karl Barth and Rudolf Bultmann, have uttered their historical skepticism and have tried to 'demystify' the Gospels. For Bultmann, the resurrection signifies that Jesus continues to survive in the preaching of his disciples. Even though they call themselves Christian, they no longer believe in Jesus' miracles. And the German theologian A.L.S. Bär has asserted that 'not the historical Jesus, but the preached Christ has become the guiding light for very many'.

Some skeptic freethinkers have even uttered the possibility that Jesus did NOT die on the cross. As stated by the swoon hypothesis, the collapsed Nazorean regained consciousness in the tomb, slid away the heavy tombstone and stumbled outside.

But if a disfigured and exhausted Jesus later showed up among his startled disciples, how could this appearance have been interpreted as a glorious resurrection? A holy conviction that some of them later paid with a frightening martyr's death.

The same holds for the possibility, already suggested at the time of the crucifixion, that it were actually the disciples who had Jesus' body disappear. But according to Matthew, Pilate had the tomb guarded by Roman sentinels and the cap stone sealed. The Evangelist also remarks that the high priests bribed the guards with silver, paying them to spread the story that they had been asleep during the alleged 'stealing' of the corpse by the disciples.

However, it is almost certain that the Evangelists did not make up the story of the empty grave. Indeed, all four Gospels mention that it were WOMEN who first saw the empty tomb. With as crown witness, of all people, Mary Magdalene, once allegedly possessed by seven demons. If one knows, moreover, that the testimony of a woman was absolutely worthless in the extremely patriarchal society of that time…

In the Gospels, by the way, there is nowhere a formal indication that this Mary of the little town of Magdala was, or had been, a prostitute. But a closer reading of the text reveals that the 'anonymous women' that had crossed Jesus' path were indeed of dubious mores and that the Magdalene was wrongly identified with them.

The most surprising thesis that lately has come from exegetic Bible analysis, states that Mary Magdalene evolved as an authoritative figure in the early Christian community. She would actually have been the real author of the Gospel of John!

Then, there are Jesus' post mortal apparitions. The stunned apostles saw their resurrected and self-confident rabbi a couple of times in Jerusalem (with doubting Thomas), at the lake of Tiberias in Galilee (where he had fish for breakfast!) and on Mount of Olives, before his Asuncion. The disciples spoke with him and touched his healed crucifixion wounds with surprise.

According to Paul, who had never met the Nazorean in his life, Jesus' glorified body appeared first to Peter, James, the apostles, and 'five hundred brothers'. At last, Jesus turned towards him in a sea of light (women were not worth mentioning for Paul, or he actually did not know them).

Nothing but hallucinations or inventions, skeptics jeer. Fair enough, it is mentioned several times in the Gospels that the resurrected Jesus was not immediately, or even not at all, recognized by his followers (cf. the story of two of his disciples walking to Emmaus).

The liberal theology is not really happy with the resurrection story, as there is also Paul's declaration that *'if Christ has not been raised, then our proclamation has been in vain and your faith has been in vain.'* (1 Corinthians 15:14)

Today, more and more frustrated believers find their way back to the miracle church of the early days. A reappraisal of the ancient resurrection belief was inevitable.

**Rapture**

Paul was a Jew of the Diaspora, born in the Hellenistic town of Tarsus in Cilicia (at that time an important center dedicated to the Mithras cult). Initially, he was a fanatic persecutor of the Christians. The rigid Pharisee found his belief in the resurrection of Christ when on the road to Damascus he was addressed by a luminous and admonishing apparition.

The historical resurrection of Jesus was later explained by Paul as a prefiguration, an archetypal image of the universal end-time resurrection, which by many in those days was expected to happen very soon.

The Apostle of the Gentiles, zealous as no other and perfectly at ease in his role of pedant moralist, explained that it was the first man, Adam, who brought death in the world by his disobedience. Initially created in the image and likeness of Him, God made 'garments of skins' for this Adam and for his wife Eve, and clothed them (Genesis 3:21).

Jesus is the redeeming second Adam (the perfect Adam from before the Fall). Indeed, *'He is the image of the Invisible God'* (Colossians 1:15), and *'He is the reflection of God's glory and the exact imprint of God's very being.'* (Hebrews 1:3)

As a 'Firstborn', Paul said, the radiant light of God's glory conquered death, and opened the way to universal resurrection and reconciliation.

The word *rapture* (Lat. *raptus,* lit. seizure, fig. ecstasy) alludes to this End Time event, when, after the seven years of tribulations, all chosen Christian believers – the living and the resurrected dead – will rise into the sky. This will be followed by the second coming of Christ.

The concept of universal resurrection, particularly popular in today's Christian End Times circles, was even taken up by the popular press at the arrival of the new millennium in the year 2000.

Particularly in the United States, some religious sects give a special interpretation of this event, and they speak of a so called 'secret rapture'. Meaning the sudden seizure (literal *disappearance)* of loyal believers from the earthly sphere.

This rapture story sounds as if written by a science fiction author, yet it is actually from the two thousand years old New Testament. The Apostle Paul formulated the concept based on his interpretation of Jesus' resurrection:

'... *For the Lord himself,*' he writes in his first letter to the Thessalonians (4:16-17), *'with a cry of command, with the archangel's call and with the sound of God's trumpet, will descend from heaven, and the dead in Christ will rise first. Then we who are alive, who are left, will be caught up in the clouds together with them to meet the Lord in the air; and so we will be with the Lord forever.'*

Such a statement clearly indicates that the first Christians believed that they could expect this resurrection day during their own lifetime.

The living will rise to heaven to live there happily ever after. Around the millennium turn, it were mostly American Christian Fundamentalists that stuck to this first, general interpretation of Paul.

According to Daniel Wojcik in the British magazine *Fortean Times* (December 1999), an entire merchandising business developed: T-shirts and car-stickers with motto's such as *'Beam me up, Jesus!'* and *'Warning – driver will abandon car in case of Rapture.'*

Television series such as *Star Trek* have influenced these End Time movements, which even connected UFO's with their religion.

The unsurpassed example of this End Time craze has been the ill-famed *Heaven's Gate* incident in San Diego, California, where in March 1997, 39 members of this sect 'cut the vital functions of their physical body', preparing themselves for access to a 'higher level'. In the wake of the passing Hale-Bopp com-et, an enormous space vessel – 'a UFO sent by God' – would pick up the besotted followers of the cult's leader Marshall Applewhite before the entire world would be destroyed (Among the individuals who committed suicide was the real-life brother of the Afro-American Lieutenant Uhura from the original *Star Trek* series.)

In the light of this bubble gum theology, one could easily dismiss the entire rapture idea as ridiculous nonsense. Only, in other letters of Paul, there are some intriguing details that he – significantly – introduces as *a mystery* (Greek: mysterion).

*'What I am saying, brothers and sisters,'* he declares in 1 Corinthian 15:50-53, *'is this: flesh and blood cannot inherit the Kingdom of God, nor does the perishable inherit the imperishable. Listen, I will tell you a mystery! We will not all die, but we will all be changed, in a moment, in the twinkling of an eye, at the last trumpet. For the trumpet will sound, and the dead will be raised imperishable, and we will be changed. For this perishable body must put on imperishability, and this mortal body must put on immortality.'*

Thus, the living will not literally ascend to the Paradise behind the clouds. Paul speaks of a transmutation of the physical body: its basic material will undergo a jump variation. An altered form of the body will enter the invisible Kingdom of God without dying.

Inevitably, we are reminded of the words and actions of Jesus the Nazorean. The following sentence discloses the basis of Paul's resurrection doctrine: the rising of Jesus from the dead.

> *'He will transform the body of our humiliation that it may be conformed to the body of his glory, by the power that also enables him to make all things subject to himself.'*
> (Philippians 3:21)

## The glorified body

It is often said that Paul's Gnostic-Hellenistic interpretation of the figure of Christ is the corner stone of actual Christianity. In any case, his resurrection doctrine is very close to a numinous or sublime incident (the Transfiguration) that is described in Mark 9:1-4:

> *'And he said to them, "Truly I tell you, there are some standing here who will not taste death until they see that the Kingdom of God has come with power* (Greek: dynamei).*"*
>
> *Six days later, Jesus took with him Peter and James and John, and led them up a high mountain apart, by themselves. And he was transfigured* (Greek: metamorphote) *before them, and his clothes became dazzling white, such as no one on earth could bleach them. And there appeared to them Elijah with Moses, who were talking with Jesus.'*

Matthew 17:2 reads:

> *'And he was transfigured before them, and his face shone like the sun, and his clothes became dazzling white.'*

And finally in Luke 9:29:

> *'And while he was praying, the appearance of his face changed, and his clothes became dazzling white.'*

It is very likely that this luminous process was the same that later activated Jesus' resurrection. According to Luke – for whom this transfiguration (on Mount Tabor) happened during the night – *'Moses and Elijah ap-*

*peared in glory and were speaking of his departure, which he was about to accomplish at Jerusalem.'*

As I previously mentioned, Jesus forbade his disciples to speak about this miraculous event, until after his resurrection (a warning that the frightened trio did not understand either).

According to Luke and John, there also stood two shining figures close by, or in, the empty tomb. For Luke these figures were men, for John they were angels *(angelous)*. This corroborates a side remark of Jesus in Matthew 22:30:
*'For at the resurrection (…) one shall be as the angels.'*

In Matthew 28, an angel of the Lord sat on the rolled-away tombstone and:
*'His appearance was like lightning, and his clothing white as snow.'*

Mark only mentions a young man in a long white robe at the empty tomb.

One can ask oneself whether these two 'angels', and 'Moses and Elijah' who appeared in their glory on Mount Tabor, were not the same figures. Figures who played a particular role in Jesus' resurrection?

Mark 15:34 mentions bystanders at the cross who thought that Jesus called the prophet Elijah, when he cried out with a loud voice:
*'Eli lama sabachtani?'* (This is translated – in Greek – by Mark as *'My God, why have you forsaken me?'*)

One interpretation could be that it was indeed Elijah who was called by Jesus, accusing him – prematurely, as would become clear three days later – of breaking his promise…

## Touch

When an excited Mary Magdalene is the first to recognize Jesus in the Garden of Gethsemane (after some hesitation; she initially took him for a gardener), he rebuffs her with the intriguing words:

*'Do not touch me, for I have not yet gone to the Father.'*

Intriguing indeed. Could this suggest that Jesus had somehow managed to reanimate his physical body – as he had done before with Lazarus, the little daughter of Jairus and the young man of Nain – but that his own 'glorification' was not yet fully completed?

Undoubtedly, there is a connection between Jesus' warning Mary Magdalene, and his earlier reprimand of a woman, who had suffered from haemorrhages for twelve years (Mark 5:25). A surprised Jesus felt his 'force' ebb away from him, as the desperate woman secretly touched the fringe of his cloak and was healed of her disease. Soon many sick people were brought to him, and they begged him that they might even touch the fringe of his cloak (Matthew 14:36).

In the case of miraculous healings, there is often (but not always) a mention of laying on hands, or another kind of direct physical contact. It is remarkable that Jesus, at all times, took his distance from his astounding interventions. He strictly ordered his disciples that no one should know what happened (Mark 5:43, Mark 7:36 and Mark 8:26).

Definitively of the same nature as the luminous metamorphosis of Jesus on Mount Tabor – and in many ways a prefiguration of it – is the bizarre incident that happened during the Jewish Exodus from Egypt.

Exodus 34:29-33 reads:

*'Moses came down from Mount Sinai. As he came down from the mountain with the two tablets of the covenant in his hand, Moses did not know that the skin of his face shone because he had been talking with God. When Aaron and all the Israelites saw Moses, the skin of his face was shining, and they were afraid to come near him (...) When Moses had finished speaking with them, he put a veil on his face.'*

The two persons that Jesus met on Mount Tabor were Moses and the prophet Elijah. The latter had met God some four centuries after Moses on the same Sinai Mountain!

The elderly Elijah later ascended in a whirlwind to heaven before the eyes of his disciple Elisha in a *'chariot of fire and horses of fire.'* (2 Kings 2:11)

The resurrected body of Jesus was his physical body (the grave was empty), transformed into – or activated by? – his glorified body. This glorified body had the supernormal properties generally attributed to ghosts (appearance in locked rooms, sudden disappearance and finally the ascending, or levitation to heaven).

The Biblical texts occasionally suggest that even some incidental bystanders witnessed the transfiguration light.

### The sown body

*'It is sown a physical body,'* Paul explains, *'it is raised a spiritual body. If there is a physical body, there is also a spiritual body (...) But it is not the spiritual that is first, but the physical, and then the spiritual. The first*

*man was from the earth, a man of dust; the second man is from heaven. Was the man of dust, so are those who are of the dust; and as is the man of heaven, so are those who are of heaven. Just as we have borne the image of the man of dust, we will also bear the image of the man of heaven.'* (1 Corinthians 15:44-49)

In Paul's own Greek words: the *soma pneumatikon* (spiritual body, also breathing body) escapes from his cocoon, the *soma psychikon* (physical body), during the resurrection.

Paul, who made his living as a tentmaker during his missionary travels, explained it with this plastic metaphor:

*'For we know that if the earthly tent we live in is destroyed, we have a building from God, a house not made with hands, eternal in the heavens. For in this tent we groan, longing to be clothed with our heavenly dwelling — if indeed, when we have taken it off we will not be found naked.'* (2 Corinthians 5:1-3)

It is not always clear whether for Paul there still are physical remains after death (the 'destroyed tent') or not. And if so, how about the 'empty' tomb of Jesus (to which Paul never alluded in his writings)?

Because it concerns indeed the same 'clothing':

*'As many of you as were baptized into Christ, have clothed yourselves with Christ.'* (Galatians 3:27)

The interesting conversation between Mary Magdalene and the alleged gardener at the rock tomb seems to indicate that the crucified Jesus did resuscitate himself physically for a short time. As if he wanted to provide the ultimate guarantee for his extraordinary spiritual claims and promises.

Here I think of the dispute that Jesus had with some scribes on the paralytic of Capernaum. When Jesus forgave the paralytic his sins, they mocked his 'arrogance'. Jesus answered:

*'For which is easier, to say, "Your sins are forgiven", or to say, "Stand up and walk"?*
*But so that you may know that the Son of Man has authority on earth to forgive sins…'*

And he said to the paralyzed man lying on the bed:
*'Stand up, take your bed and go to your home.'* (Matthew 9:1-7)

The man stood up and, to the amazement of all present, took his bed and went away.

The assertions of Paul correspond with Jesus' parable about the Kingdom of God, in which the wearing of a precious 'bridal cloth' is required (Matthew 22:12).

In the Jewish-Kabbalistic *Zohar*, a similar notion:

*When Adam was living in the Paradise, he was dressed as the saints in heaven, in a celestial cloth of light. And the good works of man on earth earn him a part of the divine light, which will cloth him when he enters the other world…'*

*'It is sown a physical body,'* Paul says, *'it is raised a spiritual body.'*

The countless parables told by Jesus on sowers, wheat grains, good seeds, mustard seeds, sourdough, vines, fruit-bearing twigs etc., become even more intriguing in this context.

Jesus foretold his imminent death and resurrection (John 12:23):

*'The hour has come for the Son of Man to be glorified.'*
And he added to this:
*'Very truly, I tell you, unless a grain of wheat falls into the earth and dies, it remains just a single grain; but if it dies, it bears much fruit.'*

## Mysteries

The Christology of Paul shows that he was familiar with the Greek and Roman Mysteries of those days. His death and resurrection concept is not only influenced by the Judaic Messiah and the mystic ideas of Jewish sects (Essenes and Alexandrian eclectics), but also by the antique Mysteries. A number of allusions in Paul's letters (written by him about twenty years after Jesus' crucifixion) even seem to indicate that he was personally initiated into such a cult.

Paul's familiarity with the esoteric Mysteries is particularly clear from his 'mysterious' salvation doctrine. Which, by the way, he started to propagate only fifteen years after his awe-inspiring vision of light on the road to Damascus.

The publicist R.E. Witt has noticed Paul's repeated use of theological terms and concepts from the Greek and Roman mysteries: *aeons, archontes, stoicheia, musterion, gnosis, sophia, dynamis* and *agape* (charity). Witt underlined that Paul, the Apostle of the Gentiles, must have seen a number of initiation temples devoted to the Hellenized Isis on his travels through Asia-Minor and Greece.

Anyway, the idea of the Mysteries and the tripartite Hellenistic concept of spirit/soul/body fitted perfectly with the Roman Catholic belief of a survival of the soul, prior to the physical resurrection at the End of Time.

Up to the present day, we can only guess as to the nature of the initiation rites of the old Mystery Cults. Betrayal of the vows of secrecy equaled an unforgivable loss of honour, and hence a death penalty.

The purpose of the Mysteries was to show the candidate mystai that their soul, or spirit, would continue to live in a serene and blissful way after their bodily death. It was believed that an uninitiated, profane man had to endure after his passing a certain time of confusion and distress in a 'dark and chaotic wasp nest'.

According to the cautious testimonies of initiated writers and philosophers of Antiquity, the initiation ritual was very convincing, touching the participant in the deepest of his being.

**Eleusis**
In contrast to the Mysteries of Attis, Dionysos, Mithras, Isis and other cults that prospered in the Old-Greek and Roman period (and which all had more or less the same numinous objective), the Mysteries of Demeter always remained connected to one geographical location. Eleusis, 30 km North West of Athens, stayed the exclusive initiation site, from the time of the legendary King Keleos of Mycenae around 1500 BCE, till 379 CE, the year the Christianized Roman Emperor Theodosius I closed the Eleusinian Mysteries by decree.

Who really was Demeter and whether she truly taught the Mysteries to Keleos and his confidants, as was told by Homer, remains an unanswered question.

But it is certain that the initiation was first a privilege only for the members of some sacred families, the rightful owners of the cult. These families claimed to possess secret religious revelations, disclosed to their illustrious ancestors in ancient times.

In the 6$^{th}$ century BCE, after the annexation of Eleusis by Athens, two important families, the Eumolpidae and the Kerykes broke this exclusivity. They admitted all free Greeks, slaves, men and women, rich or poor to the cult. Barbarians (who did not speak Greek) were initially not admitted, but this rule was changed in the Hellenistic and Roman times. Murderers and blasphemers were strictly forbidden to participate.

The Eumolpidae and Kerykes organized the ceremonies and fixed the conditions for the initiation. From their ranks came the *hierophants* or high priests and the *torchbearers,* second in rang.

The actual initiation in the highly valued, yearly Eleusinian Mysteries was executed in three steps:
1. *Legomena* (what is said)
2. *Dromena* (what is executed)
3. *Deiknumena* (what is shown)

Clement of Alexandria, initially a Platonic, later a Christian philosopher of the 2$^{nd}$ century, gave us the following, admittedly elusive, hints as to what happened during the initiation:

'*Here are the passwords for the Mysteries of Eleusis: I have fasted, I have drunk the kykeon, I have taken from the kiste, tasted and laid back in the kalathos, I have taken again from the kalathos and laid in the kiste.*'

The *kykeon* was brewed from barley flour and a sort of wild mint. *Kiste* and *kalathos* were closed and open woven baskets. The word 'tasted' suggests, according to some texts, a sort of cake made of cereals.

In his *Exhortations to the Greeks,* the converted Clement ridiculed the ritual performance of some frank episodes from the mythic life of Demeter, the Eleusinian divinity of the Earth, and her daughter Kore (Persephone). The symbolic-theatrical performance of the kidnapping of Kore by Hades, the lecherous god of the Underworld, and of Zeus's sexual intercourse with Demeter, preceded the actual initiation.

Although the Church Father from Alexandria valued the core revelations of the Mysteries, he mocked their polytheistic origin and setting. In addition, he explicitly condemned 'the absurd and immoral fables full of indecency and superstition'.

### Epopteia

What the mystai had to experience in the Eleusinian *Telesterion* (the initiation hall) on the ninth day of the religious festival, has been a subject of divergent speculations. Plutarch and others explained that it was some sort of journey to the Underworld.

A banal set-up of smart priests? Misleading paintings, puppets and a light show? Then again, the words of the late American president Abraham Lincoln come to my mind:

*'You can fool all the people some of the time, and some of the people all the time, but you cannot fool all the people all the time.'*

The significance of the Mysteries has to be found in the countless initiates who were touched in the deepest of their soul. Moreover, these initiates remained remarkably discrete, and this over a period of more than fifteen centuries!

An alternative reading is that the mystai were first offered an introductory series of confusing torments. This can be deduced from 'veiled' texts from Antiquity, though it is not always clear whether these torments actually took place in the physical world.

Next, there would follow a symbolic representation of the life after death (analogous to the wilting and reviving of the crops; hence the dedication of the cult to the Goddess of agriculture).

Nevertheless, the enthusiastic and very convincing tone of often similar innuendos indicates that the initiation rite was very alluring. The details suggest a visionary and 'crossing-border' experience.

The ancient Greek geographer Strabo (a contemporary of Jesus) wrote:

*'The secret of the Mysteries offers a majestic impression of the divinity and reminds us of her intangible nature.'*

The Greek tragedian Sophocles:

*'Three times blessed the mortals who, after having seen the Mysteries, will enter Hades's Kingdom. For only they will live, for the others there will be only suffering.'*

And the philosopher Plutarch:

*'Death and initiation are related. It begins with a wandering in darkness and on insecure or dead-ending paths. Next is a period of fear and shiver for all kinds of horrors. Finally, the traveller experiences a strange and beautiful*

*light. He enters a pure and green land, in which he discerns soft voices, sacred words and divine visions. Among this, as an initiate he walks freely…'*

*'Blessed is he among mortals who has seen this,'* is sung in the *Hymn to Demeter*, accredited to Homer. *'But whoever is uninitiated in the rites, whoever takes no part in them, will never get a share of those things, once they die, down below in the dark territories of mist.'*

The leading priest of the Mysteries, the Hierophant – literally 'he who shows the Sacred Objects' – had an enormous status. He was assured of a place of honour in Elysium. The man (occasionally a woman) needed to have a dignified appearance and a strong voice, to pronounce the religious formulas.

At the base of the statue of the honourable Hierophant Glaucos (2$^{nd}$ century CE) one can still read the following epigram:

*'Glaucos (…) displayed to all mankind the light-bringing rites of Deo* (Demeter) *for nine years, and in the tenth he went to the immortals. Verily a beautiful mystery from the blessed ones, that death is not only no evil for mortals, but that it is good.'*

It is striking to read, how similar these testimonies are with the nowadays highly publicized NDE or near-death experience (more about this in Chapter IV).

The initiation ended with the display of the Sacred Objects in the *Anaktoron* (the most holy chapel). While he pronounced the blessed words, the Hierophant showed the mystai the *hiera,* bathing in a shining light.

Plutarch maintained that this famous Eleusinian fire was even visible directly above the open roof of the Anaktoron during the initiation night!

For some initiates, this was not the end. The following year, a second grade initiation was possible in the Mysteries of Eleusis, by assisting at the *epopteia*. This is described in cryptic and still not fully understood language as *'a reaped ear of corn shown in silence'*…

### The transcendent light

Plato's dualistic theory of Forms, and his view on the origin of the human soul is for some scholars a reflection of his concealed experiences in the Telesterion. This Athens philosopher (427-347 BCE) argued that distinct earthly objects 'with the same name' have their ideal image in the world of the Ideas, visible for the human soul only before and after the mortal life.

In his dialogue *Phaedrus*, Plato compares the viewing of the ideal Forms before life with the apparitions the mystai see during the Eleusinian initiation:

*'(…) There was a time when with the rest of the happy band they saw beauty* (of the Ideas) *shining in brightness – we philosophers following in the train of Zeus, others in company with other gods; and then we beheld the beatific vision and were initiated into a mystery which may be truly called most blessed, celebrated by us in our state of innocence, before we had any experience of evils to come, when we were admitted to the sight of apparitions innocent and simple and calm and happy, which we beheld shining in pure light, pure ourselves and not yet enshrined in*

*that living tomb which we carry about, now that we are imprisoned in the body, like an oyster in his shell.'*

Thus, the initiation signified a transcendent experience, a journey of the soul in different stages towards the core of the phenomenon Man. Therefore, the Mysteries were, in the opinion of the Romanian anthropologist Mircea Eliade, related to the shamanistic rites of 'bodily separation', *'rites with roots in prehistory.'*

The Theosophist H.P. Blavatsky has put it this way:

*'In essence, it* (the epopteia) *represents this phase of divine clairvoyance, in which all that belongs to the earth disappears, the earthly face is paralyzed and the soul, free and pure, is united with his Spirit or God.'*

The Greek word *musterion* is deduced from the word *muoo* or *myelin*, which means close the eyes or the mouth.

*'(...) The Spiritual Ego,'* she writes, *'can act only when the personal Ego is paralyzed.'*

With *'his Spirit or God'* the Russian occultist refers to the Individual Spiritual Ego (the Father of Jesus?), overshadowed by the so called Universal Spirit. According to the Theosophists, the Spiritual Ego assimilates all previous incarnations of the Personal Ego.

But how were the eyes and the mouth of the mystai closed, before the final confrontation with their Spiritual Ego? From where came the sudden 'divine clairvoyance' in the Telesterion?

H.P. Blavatsky:

*'(...) The Hierophants and some Brahmans are accused of having administered to their epoptai strong drinks or anesthetics to produce visions which shall be taken by the*

*latter as realities. They did and do use sacred beverages which, like the Soma-drink, possess the faculty of freeing the astral form from the bonds of matter; but in those visions there is as little to be attributed to hallucination as in the glimpses which the scientist, by the help of his optical instrument, gets into the microscopic world.'*

**Ergot**

In 1968, the famous mycologist R. Gordon Wasson identified the mysterious Plant-God Soma from the Old Indian *Rig Veda* hymns as *Amanita muscaria* (better known as fly amanita). Until recently, this hallucinogenic (or rather psychoactive) mushroom was used during Shamanistic rituals in Northern Siberia. Wasson introduced the term *entheogen* for all psychotropic plants eaten during ritual ceremonies in order to reach mystical ecstasy. *Entheogen* literally means 'which induces an inner manifestation of God'.

During the second International Conference on Hallucinogenic Mushrooms, in Washington, October 1977, Gordon Wasson, the classicist Carl A.P. Ruck and the Swiss biochemist Albert Hofmann gave a joint lecture. In their presentation they suggested that the hallucinogenic substance used during the Great Eleusinian Mysteries (substance to which, as already mentioned, H.P. Blavatsky had alluded a century before), was identified as *Claviceps purpurea,* the so called Ergot fungus.

They found that this parasitic fungus on ears of rye and related cereal plants produced an alkaloid, chemically related to LSD (lysergic acid diethylamide). The 'psychedelic' substance would allegedly have been mixed in small quantities with the *kykeon* or rye bread, offered to the mystai before their actual initiation (cf. Clement of Alexandria).

No wonder then that the goddess of agriculture, Demeter (Lat. *Ceres,* cereals), presided the secret cult in Eleusis!

**Salutary dazzle**
The outcome? Presumably an NDE-like trip. A two-way journey to the afterlife. Through a postmortem universe, surprisingly similar to the one described in the *Tibetan Book of the Dead.*

So, no way, life is not finished after our physical death! As the initiated Plato writes:

*'(…) pure ourselves and not yet enshrined in that living tomb which we carry about, now that we are imprisoned in the body, like an oyster in his shell.'*

The mystes sees chaotic and unstable figures, terrifying 'demons'.

*'In all initiations and Mysteries,'* the Neoplatonist Proclus writes, *'the gods exhibit many forms of themselves, and sometimes indeed an unfigured Light of themselves is held forth to the view; sometimes this Light is figured according to human form, and sometimes it proceeds into a different shape. Some of the figures are not gods and excite alarm.'*

The 3$^{rd}$ century philosopher Plotinus:

*'Thus far of the beauties of the realm of sense, images and shadow-pictures, fugitives that have entered into Matter – to adorn, and to ravish, where they are seen.'* (cf. the so called Bardo illusions of the Tibetan Book of the Dead and the distressing NDE-experiences)

And he proceeds to say:

*'(...) you should leave all such things behind and not look, but close your eyes and awaken another sort of vision instead -- a sort of vision which everyone possesses but few make use of...'*

*'(...) we must ascend again towards the Good, the desired of every Soul. Anyone that has seen This, knows what I intend when I say that it is beautiful. Even the desire of it is to be desired as a Good. To attain it is for those that will take the upward path, who will set all their forces towards it, who will divest themselves of all that we have put on in our descent. So, to those that approach the Holy Celebrations of the Mysteries, there are appointed purifications and the laying aside of the garments worn before, and the entry in nakedness – until, passing, on the upward way, all that is other than the God. Each in the solitude of himself shall behold that solitary-dwelling Existence, the Apart, the Unmingled, the Pure, that from Which all things depend, for Which all look and live and act and know, the Source of Life and of Intellection and of Being.'*

And this Existence – the Spiritual Ego of today's Theosophists – appears as a dazzling Light (cf. the primal Clear Light of the Tibetan Book of the Death).

*'When the spirit sees this divine light,'* Plotinus said, *'You wonder where it came from: from the inside or the outside world. Then, when it disappears, you say: it was from the inside. And yet, no, it was not from the inside... For in the spiritual world everything dazzles, even he who then beholds it* (cf. Jesus' contact with God's Kingdom on Mount Tabor, and his subsequent Transfiguration).

This salutary dazzle by the famous 'Eleusinian Fire' was essential during the initiation in the Telesterion.

Was it just the sunlight that the Hierophant, by opening the curtains of the Anaktoron, abruptly let into the dark space? Some skeptic historians have seriously considered this possibility. Personally, I think that such an act would only result in pain to the eyes…

# IV

# THE NEAR-DEATH EXPERIENCE

By the mid-twentieth century, it became clear to certain American academics that the allusions made by the Greek and Roman authors to the Mysteries had strong similarities with the modern reports on near-death experiences (NDE).

The antique and classic Mysteries, the rediscovered near-death experience and the Turin Shroud have the following elements in common: death, Sublime Light and rebirth...

In 1936, the British traveller-philosopher Paul Brunton spent a night in the alleged tomb of the Pharaoh Cheops, the 45 m high Great Pyramid of Giza, near Cairo. Initially, gruesome ghosts and dreary visions harassed Brunton in the dark, but after a while, his spirit came into contact with two Old-Egyptian priests. One of them told Brunton that the mysterious empty sarcophagus in the central room once had served as a temporary coffin for the candidate-initiate in the Mysteries of Osiris. In the casket, he would have experienced a sensation, which also Brunton, lying on the granite floor, gradually became aware of:

'body separation', or the progressive detachment of his personal Ego from his physical body.

In his book *A Search in Secret Egypt,* Paul Brunton compared his psychic adventure with the story of a former Air Force officer. During the war, the man underwent an operation under narcosis. Suddenly he felt himself floating in the air above the operation table, looking down on his injured body with a certain indifference.

Brunton stressed how life-changing such an experience had been for himself, and for the officer.

**Core Experiences**
Medical progress has enabled, since more than half a century, to reanimate many persons who were presumed to be clinically dead. Reanimation needs to be performed within the first ten minutes after cessation of brain function. Ten to twenty per cent of individuals who have thus escaped death, report of a short, yet far-reaching and sublime adventure 'outside the body'. In 1975, the American physician and lecturer in philosophy Raymond Moody published a collection of these testimonies in what was to become his bestseller *Life after Life.*

Moody stated that the average scenario of an NDE can be split into five successive common phases or core experiences. The persons tell how they suddenly perceive their body from an outside position and how they look down on it from a certain height. The consciousness remains clear, hearing and seeing are not affected. But pain and discomfort are substituted by an unknown, euphoric feeling of bliss (occasionally preceded, as in the case of Paul Brunton, by horrific visions).

Many experience the abrupt sensation of being sucked at high speed into a tunnel, sometimes accompanied by white 'angel-like' creatures (This tunnel sensation can also occur before the out-of-body experience.) At the other end of the tunnel, often a paradisiac landscape appears, imbued in an awe-inspiring, not blinding white light. This light, usually identified with God, is radiating an immense sense of love. Overwhelming feelings of ecstatic joy and deep emotion are reported. Now and then deceased family members are present close by.

Some individuals see and/or relive, in a timeless moment and as in a panoramic view, their entire past life, three-dimensionally and with the most trivial details. Occasionally, there is a precognition of future events…

A life-saving intervention on the physical body abruptly puts an end to the experience, generally to great discontent of the NDEr!

The organization IANDS (International Association for Near-Death Studies) cautions against simplifications. Although the near-death experiences are overall of a similar nature, they vary in their peculiarities. In its causes, manifestations, and consequences, the phenomenon is quite complex.

As Paul Brunton already noticed, the occurrence can be so overwhelmingly positive, that the experiencer later remembers it with profound nostalgia. It is a fact that the fear of death has disappeared after most NDEs.

And perhaps less trivial than it may seem at first: most persons who have lived an NDE finally consider *'charity'* as their ultimate goal in life…

## Susan Blackmore

The results of a George Gallup Jr. Poll from 1995, showed that about 12 million citizens of the United States of America had lived a near-death experience. Neither race, gender, social status nor religion played a determining role.

Medical doctors have concluded that not all these stories can be dismissed as fabrications. Yet most physicians do not consider the NDE as a proof of a personal afterlife. They note that lack of oxygen in the brain can elicit euphoric hallucinations of the same nature as a psychedelic trip.

I am not certain that she is pleased with it, but hardcore skeptics of the CSI *(Committee for Skeptical Inquiry,* formerly CSICOP), often cite the British psychologist and ex-parapsychologist Susan Blackmore, as the expert spokesperson of the so called brain-death theory (in contrast to the afterlife theory).

As a student, Blackmore had an out-of-body experience herself, while smoking a *joint*. She wrote two skeptical books on the subject, books frequently cited in the NDE literature: *Beyond the Body* (1982) and *Dying to Live* (1993).

Blackmore makes a distinction between the actual, authentic experience and the interpretation (or conceptualization) often given to it by the near-death experiencer: the separation of a subtle body double, or so called astral projection (AP).

The occult notion of astral projection is very old and known all over the world. In the West, the theory was especially popularized around 1900 by the oriental doctrines of the Theosophical Society. Around that time, the notorious magic society *The Golden Dawn* taught its British members a number of techniques to 'catapult' their astral body to a more subtle plane or realm of existence.

For the Theosophists, the utter or absolute reality (as well as man) is composed of a series of planes of varying consistency, from which the material elements are successively eliminated. These different levels interpenetrate each other. Our five physical senses can only discern the coarse physical plane. The substance of the second, astral plane (closest to the physical) is thinner than the most airy gases from our everyday environment.

As maintained by the occult doctrines, our individual feelings and thoughts determine largely this partially personal, partially shared astral plane.

Following the physical death of the body, the more subtle astral body dissociates itself from the terrestrial one, whereafter the displaced 'self' starts a visionary journey through ever thinner planes. According to the astral projection model, a person experiencing an NDE becomes, for a short period of time, acquainted with this post-mortem state.

**Astral travellers**

Psychologists such as Charles Tart and Karl Osis had already performed physiological experiments with elicited out-of-body experiences (OBEs, the most common feature of NDEs) before the sensational publication by Raymond Moody. Indeed, an OBE can be an independent phenomenon, not necessarily linked to a critical, life-threatening situation.

A number of expert astral travellers caught the world's attention with their bestselling books, giving records of their unusual exploits. The Americans Sylvan Muldoon and Robert Monroe, the British Oliver Fox and the South-African mathematician J.H.M. Whiteman often agree with each other on the possibilities of their skills, and their declarations correspond in general with the Theosophical doctrines.

In details, they can differ. Thus, some describe a silver 'astral cord' connecting the physical with the astral body. Others do not mention this cord at all. Nor such a thing as an etheric or an astral body, that would be a subtle duplicate of the physical body. Some experience their OBE as just an out-of-body displacement of their view angle.

Most people who experience an OBE declare that the 'physical' world they perceive from this new point of view is not entirely the same as the one they are used to. It is more a sort of 'find the seven mistakes' copy. The colour of the wallpaper may differ, or the doorknob of their room may be missing. There may be a metallic cupboard instead of a wooden one, etc.

The initial lab experiments aiming to demonstrate an extrasensory perception (ESP) during elicited OBEs, resulted, time and again, in a frustrating combination of correct and flawed observations. Perhaps some of this can be reconciled with the occult speculations on the deceitful nature of the astral plane and its mixed shared and individual content.

These and other characteristics – such as the sensation of flying, the easy displacement to a new location, the impression of a 'more real than life' environment – suggest that there is a connection of an OBE with the more frequently occurring lucid dream, in which the dreamer is actually conscious of the fact that he is dreaming.

The skeptic reduces the OBE to the experience of a lucid dream. But he overlooks those practised lucid dreamers who declare that such dreams are of a completely different nature than the OBE's they have occasionally experienced as well.

On the other hand, it is not excluded that there is a link between the delusive familiar surroundings that a dreamer experiences during a so called 'false awakening' and the familiar surroundings encountered during an OBE. Oliver Fox asserted that it is even fairly easy to elicit an OBE from such a false awakening.

Corroborating occult doctrines, a number of famous OBErs claim to have been in contact with different planes (and their 'inhabitants') that range from the more or less familiar to the outright mystical ones.

**Stable model**
Susan Blackmore has argued that the astral projection theory of an OBE is too elaborate and too adaptable to be called scientific. Her view is the following:

Under normal circumstances, the five senses and the brain present a stable model of the outer world to the consciousness. This model is perceived as consistent, communal and hence as 'objective'. Still, if the brain is confronted with oxygen shortage or overstimulation, a partial, or even a complete information stop through the senses can occur. A model based on personal memory content and imagination then takes over from the 'objective' model. The self-consciousness, still intact, experiences this 'false' reality (often observed from a bird perspective) as misleadingly objective.

The well-known tunnel vision experienced during an NDE, is for Blackmore the result of a disturbance in the visual cortex of the brain. The life review is the outcome of an overstimulation of the temporary lobes, in which memories are stored. An overproduction of pain-killing endorphins would induce the euphoric, often mystical sensation.

Susan Blackmore (who, by the way, practised meditation for more than twenty years), has come to this conclusion:

*'World and self are merely the construction (models) of an information processing system (the brain) and therefore – like Buddha said – an illusion.'*

It is a fact that original Buddhism sometimes is hardly distinguishable from Western atheism and physicalism. Buddhism, however, has the concept of rebirth. In contrast to Hinduism, Buddhism rejects the existence of a permanent 'self' or Ego. What is reincarnated in Buddhism is a karma-driven 'stream of consciousness' (whatever that may be).

The difference between the Zen-reality of Blackmore and the near-death experience lies in the fact that in the latter a personal, not a shared illusion is involved.

Remains the question of the often similar, coherent, and outspokenly *ethical* nature of these experiences.

Moreover, if this out-of-body experience is only a subjective sensation, how then explain the well-documented and certified 'remote viewing' reported during some NDEs? And what about the occasional effective manipulation of physical objects from a distance (psycho- or telekinesis)?

Questions that have led to the parapsychological theory: an out-of-body experience is actually the sum of imagination and clairvoyance and/or telekinesis.

Skeptics dismiss psychokinesis as irrational and reduce the alleged remote viewing to *cryptomnesia,* when a forgotten memory returns without it being recognized as such. The skeptic psychobiophysical theory classifies the rest as hallucinations, disturbances of the proprioception (or somatic sense) caused by a short circuit in the neuronal network.

And what about the compassionate and sublime feelings experienced during an NDE? For some they are nothing more than an evolutionary acquired process of misleading, aiming to accept the pending brain death without too much protest!

**Ketamine**

In 1995, the psychiatrist and pharmacologist Karl L.R. Jansen from New Zealand proposed the ketamine model of the near-death experience.

During cell death caused by lack of oxygen, glutamate binds massively to the NMDA-receptors on the neurons of the pre-cortex, the temporal lobes and the hippocampus. A (hypothetical) neuroprotective defence mechanism is put in place, resulting in the production of endopsychosines, which will block the threatened NMDA receptors. And this may elicit hallucinatory effects in individuals in whom the input from the senses is interrupted.

Jansen asserted that a same NDE-like experience can be induced in patients and volunteers who are anesthetized with *ketamine*, a molecule that also binds to the NMDA receptors: out-of-body sensation, vision of a tunnel, the Light, a feeling of euphoria, remembrance of one's life in retrospect, etc.

In contrast to Susan Blackmore, Karl Jansen gradually became convinced that during a spontaneous (or triggered) NDE, these hallucinations have a spiritual ontological quality. In his paper *Ketamine (K) and Quantum Psychiatry* (1999) Jansen states that it is possible that both on ketamine and during an NDE there is a re-tuning of the brain that will allow the 'self' to come into contact with an actual transcendental dimension.

It was already known that some of the core experiences of an NDE could be elicited 'artificially'. Mid of the twentieth century, the Canadian neurosurgeon Wilder Penfield stimulated, under local anaesthesia, the temporal brain cortex or lobes of patients suffering from partial epilepsy, with weak electrical impulses (three volt). Some patients were suddenly confronted, visually and/or auditory, with remarkably vivid, albeit fragmented and random episodes from their past. Others heard heavenly music and/or had the feeling to lose contact with their body *('Oh God! I am leaving my body.')*.

Besides, these same sensations can also occur during spontaneous epileptic discharges.

In the opinion of the American paediatrician and NDE-expert Melvin Morse, a place in the right temporal lobe, named by him the *God Spot,* plays an essential role in the near-death experience. The complex, ordered and consistent nature of these so-called 'illusionary' reactions is often striking.

Let us now hear what the Dutch writer/poet and former ketamine-user Hans Plomp had to say. Plomp confirmed that his experiences were often similar to NDE-testimonies (the tunnel, mystical figures, and feelings of cosmic unification). In contrast to the, admittedly important, neurobiological conclusions of pharmacologist Karl Jansen, Hans Plomp gave a personal and very poignant report of his ketamine-experience:

*'There is consciousness without the body, there is "life" after "death", there exist other "higher" beings in the universe, while living we can be initiated in the enigmas of the mysteries. To find the confirmation of my deepest hope gave me a feeling of ecstasy, that one can hardly imagine in the "daily reality".'*

From all this, it must be clear that two categorically different opponents are fighting the querulous NDE-debate. One could say that Plomp speaks about the (inter) subjective, meaningful musical universe of Beethoven's Ninth Symphony. And Jansen about the objective interaction between bows and string instruments, that brings to life an entrancing and profoundly human symphony that already exists on an invisible plane.

**Pim van Lommel**

The seminal paper *NDE in survivors of cardiac arrest: a prospective study in the Netherlands* (December 2001) of the Dutch cardiologist Pim van Lommel and his collaborators summarized the results of a research performed on 344 patients, diagnosed as clinically dead, who had been reanimated following a cardiac arrest. Sixty-two of them reported a near-death experience, among whom at least forty-one described one of the core experiences.

Having an NDE was not related to the duration of the cardiac arrest or unconsciousness. Nor with the seriousness of the case or with previous feelings of fear by the patient. Importantly, no physiological or neurophysiological signals could be identified that had triggered the NDE.

*'We do not know why so few patients report an NDE after their reanimation,'* van Lommel wrote in the medical journal *The Lancet*.

*'(…) If a purely physiological explanation, such as oxygen deficiency, would be the cause, one would expect that most patients would report an NDE after reanimation from their clinical death.'*

Two and eight years later, the survivors still had a sharp memory of their transcendent adventure. Most persons also had undergone a personality change, especially on a 'spiritual' and 'intuitive' level.

The conclusion of Dr van Lommel is remarkable:

*'With lack of evidence for any other theory for NDE, the thus far assumed, but never proven, concept that consciousness and memories are localised in the brain should be discussed. How could a clear consciousness outside one's body be experienced at the moment that the brain no longer functions during a period of clinical death with flat EEG? (…)'*

**Ritual resurrection**

Pim van Lommel briefly mentioned in his *Lancet* paper a publication on a much-discussed research of 'seeing' by blind individuals during an NDE: the book *Mindsight, Near-Death and Out-of-Body Experiences in the Blind* (1999) of the American psychologist Kenneth Ring.

Ring, affiliated to Connecticut University and co-founder of the international NDE foundation IANDS, had read Paul Brunton's experience in the Great Pyramid. In 1984, he published in *Anabiosis* – at that time the official IANDS journal – a study on Brunton's adventure. In the paper, Ring proposed that the Old-Egyptian Mysteries of Osiris in fact elicited artificially near-death experiences (the original Egyptian title of the *Egyptian Book of the Dead* is indeed *per tem rhu*, or *Book of Coming Forth by Day*, also translated as *Book of Emerging Forth into the Light*).

The previous year, another IANDS member, Michael Grosso of Jersey City State College, had already made the link, in the same journal, with the far better known Old-Greek Mysteries (of Old-Egyptian origin, according to many writers in Antiquity).

The improved medical reanimation techniques accidentally brought the NDE's within the reach of many.

Dr Michael Grosso warns:

*'One place where the ancient archetype of the Western Overself returns with all the force of the repressed, is the hospital deathbed. Amid the scene of ritual resuscitation where, unfortunately, there are no Hierophants, no guides, no one to help tease out the meaning of the expe-*

*rience from the afterglow of memory, there the mythology of death and enlightenment comes to life, powerful as old, flashing with transforming light, the heights and the abysses all intact.*

*But probably for the great majority, and it would seem we are talking of millions of patients now, one has to say with T. S. Eliot, "We had the experience but missed the meaning".*

*Near-death researchers are helping to resuscitate the meaning and to decipher the Rosetta stone of the psyche's ancient mysteries (…).'*

## Wisdom for the Perfects

Occultists, parapsychologists and some alert physicians have made the link between the concealed experiences of the mystai, the astral projection and the near-death experience.

To recapitulate the most frequently occurring sensations of an NDE:

The out-of-body experience, with the subtle body (etheric double, spirit, soul) leaving the physical body and observing the latter from above.

The fact of being sucked into a dark tunnel or a constricted passage.

The confrontation at the other end of the tunnel with a dazzling and sublime (numinous) white light.

Let us compare these sensations with the following words of the Apostle Paul that – added to his obsession for the Transfiguration – lead to the assumption that he himself had been initiated (though he kept this secret). A (not always so) modest Paul speaks here of himself in the third person:

> *'I know a person in Christ who fourteen years ago was caught up to the third heaven — whether in the body or out of the body I do not know; God knows. And I know that such a person — whether in the body or out of the body I do not know; God knows — was caught up into Paradise and heard things that are not to be told, that no mortal is permitted to repeat.'* (2 Corinthians, 12:2-4)

I have mentioned before, how Paul often expressed himself in his letters in specific Greek terms. Since its conquest by Alexander the Great, Palestine and its surroundings had undergone a strong Hellenistic influence. There is no doubt that Paul's knowledge of the Greek language was impeccable. A certain vocabulary indicates that his interpretation of Jesus' death and resurrection was actually coloured by what he had experienced during a non-Jewish initiation rite.

This perplexed, but obsessive searcher was apparently not too shy to draw from unorthodox wells. Probably, Paul had sought initiation out of curiosity and frustration, intrigued by the dying and resurrecting God-Saviour of the pagan Mysteries. It would seem that his salvation theology, focused on the figure of Christ, took its final form after he had been initiated and seen the very same Light that had overwhelmed him before on the road to Damascus…

Like Jesus, Paul speaks about the 'wisdom that can only be spoken by the Perfects' and about 'things that are not to be told'. With these words he does not differ from Jesus, who spoke to the people in parables and kept the secrets of the Kingdom of God for his (apparently hard of hearing) Apostles.

We cannot formally prove that the Apostle of the Gentiles was initiated into the Eleusinian Mysteries, in the immensely popular Mysteries of Isis or in another Hellenistic cult of that time. Yet the words of the Greek mystes Plotinus, that I have already cited before, surely sound very much like Paul's in 2 Corinthians, 12:2-4:

*'When the spirit sees this divine light,'* Plotinus wrote, *'You wonder where it came from: from the inside or the outside world. Then, when it disappears, you say: it was from the inside. And yet, no, it was not from the inside... For in the spiritual world everything dazzles, even he who then beholds it.'*

I now want to repeat two passages that are unmistakably and intriguingly connected with each other:
1. *'A physical body is sown and a spiritual body is resuscitated.'* (cf. Jesus' parables of the sowers, the grain, the good seeds, mustard seed, etc.)

*'The hour has come for the Son of Man to be glorified.'*

Jesus predicts his forthcoming death and resurrection (John 12:23).

And he adds:

*'Very truly, I tell you, unless a grain of wheat falls into the earth and dies, it remains just a single grain; but if it dies, it bears much fruit.'*

2. A year after the initiation in the 'Eleusinian Fire' of the Anaktoron, the mystes could get access to the highest grade of initiation: the *epopteia*. During this second initiation he was given the formal proof of a glorious life after his physical death. Hippolytus of Rome, a Church

Father of the second century CE, described the *epopteia* as *'a reaped ear of corn shown in silence'*...

From what followed thereafter, we remember especially the rest of this text by the same Hippolytus:

*'At night in Eleusis, the Hierophant appearing in the midst of many fires, proclaims the great and secret mystery, saying: "The Holy Brimo (Kore) has borne a sacred child, Brimos," that is, the mighty has borne the mighty. For sublime, he said, is the spiritual or what is formed above, and therefore mighty is what thus is formed.'*

Hippolytus's informant, a gnostic Naassene, compared the initiated epoptes with *'bridegrooms, emasculated by a virginal spirit. This virgin carries and gives birth to a son, not animal nor of the flesh, but for ever blessed'*...

**Golden Flower**

There is a remarkable similarity between the previous ideas and the 'meditation technique' developed in a Chinese-Taoist tractate.

*The Secret of the Golden Flower* offers an orally transmitted doctrine from the 8$^{th}$ century. These teachings – the so called 'religion of the golden life-elixir' – were told by the legendary Taoist philosopher of that time Lü Yen.

In 1920, the German missionary and sinologist Richard Wilhelm sent his translation of the *Golden Flower* to his friend Carl Gustav Jung. The Swiss analyst discovered in the book many symbols, familiar to him from the dreams of his patients. It influenced his ideas concerning autonomous psychic functions and archetypal images and had him place these in a broader context.

The exceptional Chinese manual speaks about an immortal 'golden flower' (or 'flower of Light' or 'diamond body') that can be sown and harvested through meditation. The development of an 'immortal embryo' requires special breathing techniques as well as the control of sexual and other physiological energies.

Jung saw in the *Golden Flower* a symbolic description of what he called the process of individuation: the transformation of the conditioned 'I' into the free Self.

Or:

*'The translocation of the psychical nucleus of the 'I' to a transpersonal instance, made up of soul and spirit.'*

Jung also discovered the imagery of the *Secret of the Golden Flower* in many Western manuscripts on alchemy. Which seemed to confirm an esoteric truth: the transmutation of base metals into gold and the fabrication of the Life-elixir paralleled the 'ennoblement process' of the alchemist in *person*. The most important tool required for all this, was an extremely activated fantasy or *imagination*. As maintained by Jung, the technique was based on the notion (also suggested nowadays by a number of quantum physicists) that matter and spirit are of the same nature. Both would be the explicit manifestations of an underlying 'psychoid' unity.

Many assertions in the Chinese *Golden Flower* show parallels with the claims of the Jews Jesus and Paul concerning the rebirth. This has puzzled several academics. As noticed by translator Richard Wilhelm, also in the *Golden Flower* the Light (the Flower) refers to the life of the human beings.

*'Man is spiritually reborn out of water and fire,'* Wilhelm says, *'to which must be added thought-earth (*spirit*), as womb, or tilled field.'*

As stated by a bold hypothesis, the Christian Nestorians travelled to China and Mongolia in the 7$^{th}$ century and marked their stamp on the esoteric transfiguration doctrine of the Taoist *Golden Flower*.

The 5$^{th}$ century Byzantine patriarch Nestorius had made a distinction between Jesus Christ's human personality and his inner Divine Logos. With his heretic point of view, Nestorius opposed the official Unitarian doctrine and for safety reasons, he emigrated with his disciples to the East. The Nestorian doctrine was known in China as the *Jingjiào* or 'shining religion'.

Some Western historians even think that the Taoist sage Lü Yen converted to Nestorianism!

# V

# THE HOLY SPIRIT

According to 1 Peter 3:18, the holy spirit *(pneuma agion)* is of the same nature as Jesus' transfiguration- or resurrection body. In his letter to the Romans, Paul explains that Christ's inner spirit activated the revitalisation of his physical body. Every human being can hope for this resurrection if God's or Christ's spirit lives in him/her.

In 2 Corinthians 3:16-18, this eloquent convert from 'the important city' of Tarsus (who suddenly considered the Judaic Books of the Law as obsolete) points to a completely inversed relationship between man and God. The text makes a link between the holy spirit and the glorified man:

*'But when one turns to the Lord, the veil is removed. Now the Lord is the Spirit, and where the Spirit of the Lord is, there is freedom. And all of us, with unveiled faces, seeing the glory of the Lord as though reflected in a mirror, are being transformed into the same image from one degree of glory to another; for this comes from the Lord, the Spirit.'*

The so called baptism with the spirit, or the receiving of the spirit, is an essential condition to be part of the glory of Christ.

A correct understanding of this mysterious holy spirit will bring us a step closer to the true origin of the Turin Shroud...

For the Roman Catholics, the Holy Spirit is the Third Person of the Divine Trinity. But for the Jews and for many Christian splinter groups, the *pneuma agion* of the New Testament is the same as the impersonal *ruah* of the Old Testament (i.e. God's breathing, spirit, life force, also wind). This ruah provokes visions, inspires prophets and is the driving force of all sorts of paraphysical and parapsychological phenomena.

It is this 'energy' that activated the numerous miracles performed by Jesus.

A moving example is the story of the woman who had suffered for twelve years from bleedings. This incident, as told by Mark 5:25-34, must be authentic and it merits once more our attention. The events reveal the specific relation that Jesus had with his own 'force'.

The woman secretly touched the fringes – *titzit* or tassels, attached following the Jewish tradition – of his garment, and she was *instantly* healed. Jesus, who suddenly felt a loss of his 'force', looked behind him and insistently asked who had touched him. Even his disciples were surprised.

*'You see the crowd pressing in on you; how can you say, "Who touched me"?'*

The frightened woman came forward and told her sad story. And Jesus replied:

*'Daughter, your faith has made you well; go in peace, and be healed of your disease.'*

Apparently the woman had been cured by a spontaneous 'energetic' reaction, not by Jesus' authority. Probably not coincidental, Jesus, at that very moment, had been accompanying a desperate Jairus to his house. This presiding servant of the local synagogue had begged Jesus to save his dying daughter…

But when Jesus, during his tumultuous arrest on the Mount of Olives, healed a high priest's slave, whose right ear had been cut off by Peter, this was indeed an intentional act from his side, which had nothing to do with the faith of the shocked victim (Luke 22:51).

**The other helper**
In John 14:26, Jesus announces the coming of the Holy Spirit, which he also calls 'the other helper' *(parakletos)*, invisible to the world. He stresses that he cannot send this inspiring helper before his own resurrection.

Jehovah's Witnesses, for instance, see the parakletos as a mere linguistic personification. This Christian denomination compares (perhaps correctly) this invisible active force of God with electromagnetic waves or a sort of nuclear energy.

Ten days after Jesus' ascension to heaven, when the day of Pentecost had come, the following happened:
*'And suddenly from heaven there came a sound like the rush of a violent wind, and it filled the entire house where they were sitting. Divided tongues, as of fire, appeared among them, and a tongue rested on each of them. All of them were filled with the Holy Spirit and began to speak in other languages, as the Spirit gave them ability.'*
(Acts 2: 2-4)

A little parenthesis.

The Pentecost incident shows similarities with some paranormal stunts of the famous 19th century Scottish medium Daniel Dunglas Home.

Arguably the most amazing figure in history besides Jesus, Dunglas Home is reported to have flown out of a spiritualist séance room through a window and to have floated in again, a little later, through another window! The young Lord Adare, then army officer and war correspondent, and his friend Lord Lindsay, later a member of the *Royal Society* and president of the *Royal Astronomical Society*, were witness of this *tour de force*.

During this same séance, Adare saw above the head of Home *a bird appearing out of nowhere, fiery tongues and flames*. Moreover, they heard a sound of a strong wind, as maintained by Lord Adare *'the weirdest thing I ever heard'*…

In 1 Corinthian 12:8-10, Paul lists a number of Spirit gifts: wisdom, knowledge, healing power, prophesizing, speaking in foreign languages, discernment of spirits, and working of miracles.

He alludes to the same 'force' that activated Christ's miracles, and of which he spoke in his promise to the Apostles in Acts 1:8.

*'(…) But you will receive power* (dynamin) *when the Holy Spirit has come upon you (…)'*

Apparently, that power must have been very convincing. In Acts 8:18 we read that a certain Simon 'who previously had practised magic and astounded the people of Samaria', was speechless when he saw 'the signs and great miracles' that the Apostle Philip performed. Immediately, many Samarians and also Simon had themselves baptized by Philip in the name of Jesus.

When the Apostles in Jerusalem heard about Philip's success, they sent Peter and John to the Samarian converts to lay their hands on them and thereby giving them the Holy Spirit. Simon the magician, impressed by the practice, offered them money:

*'Give me also this power so that anyone on whom I lay my hands may receive the Holy Spirit.'*

Upon which an outraged Peter threatened Simon.

This story shows the clear difference between the traditional baptism with water (washing of the sins) and the mystical baptism with the Holy Spirit, a novelty unheard-of so far. Apparently, the baptism with the Holy Spirit (by laying on of hands) could only be given by two of the three confidants of Jesus, who had witnessed his Transfiguration on Mount Tabor (Peter, John and James).

Both the Hebrew term *ruah* and the Greek word *pneuma* (Latin: *spiritus)* are thus associated, on the one hand, with (re)generative and paranormal skills, and on the other hand with luminous and marvelous phenomena.

More or less synonymous with these terms are the notions *doxa* (magnificence) and *eikon* in the New Testament: the visible, glorious presence of God or the Sublime. And also with the notion *Kabod* in the Old Testament and the Talmudic *Shekinah:* light phenomena, burning bramble bush, columns of fire, etc.

In Philip 3:21, the resurrection body of Christ is called *soma tes doxes.* 1 Corinthians 15:43 stresses that it is raised in power.

The old Church Fathers have speculated in their writings on the qualities of Jesus' and of our future resurrection body. Paul asserts that it is subtle, imperishable, radiant and powerful.

## Judeo-Christians

The first disciples of Jesus the Nazorean gathered in Jerusalem, as a sectarian group with a distinct interpretation of the Messiah figure. However, it goes without saying that the group continued to respect the old Mosaic laws. The Apostle Peter and later Jesus' brother James were its first leaders.

According to church historian Eusebius, these so called Judeo-Christians left Jerusalem before the destruction of the Temple by the Romans (CE 70). They settled in Pella, one of the ten Hellenistic cities of Dekapolis, east of the river Jordan. The group later returned to Jerusalem and had as new spokesperson Simeon, son of Cleophas (this Simeon, according to most Christian traditions, was the second Bishop of Jerusalem). These early Christians, who still practised circumcision, split in the course of time in different sects, with divergent understandings of the figure of Jesus.

Paul, who was in favour of a radical abolition of the Mosaic ritual precepts, fulminated at times against Jesus' first disciples. He wanted to bring the Good Message (at least his personal view on it) also to the people who were not circumcised.

The Lord, as stated by Paul, had, by his death and resurrection, rendered superfluous the cumbersome religious customs of the Old Covenant; only the belief in the reconciling power of Christ's sacrifice was now beatific.

Paul's letters testify of his frantic attempts to break with the early church of Jerusalem. This even resulted in an overt confrontation with Peter. In 2 Galatians, Paul accuses Peter, who is called here by his original Aramaic name Kephas, of a double-crossing attitude towards pagans and circumcised.

Peter on the other hand, used a scathing language against certain teachers and false prophets (at least in 2 Peter, a letter of which the authenticity is also disputed). Although, a little further, he seems to accept Paul's authority, Peter complains about his obscure statements that could lead to confusion.

After the Second Jewish Revolt (CE 135), uncircumcised bishops became the leaders of the community of Jerusalem. This resulted in even more discord between Judeo-Christians and non-Jewish converts. The former (Nazoreans and Ebionites) were finally in the 4$^{th}$ century dismissed as fools and excommunicated by the, by then, well organised and triumphant Pauline (Roman Catholic) Church.

**Baptism**
In Matthew 3:11, John the Baptist baptizes with water. He who will come after him (i.e. Jesus), the Baptist says, will baptize with the holy spirit and fire. Yet, according to John 3:22 and 4:1, Jesus and his followers also baptized with water (the sentence 2 – *'although it was not Jesus himself but his disciples who baptized'* – seems to be added later).

A similar contradiction between Acts 19:2-7 and John 1:33-34.

In Ephesus, Paul learns from two disciples that they have been baptized by the itinerant preacher Apollos with the baptism of John. They have never heard of a holy spirit (Acts 19:2-7). Yet, John the Baptist had received, some twenty years earlier, God's instruction when he baptized Jesus:

*'I myself did not know him, but the one who sent me to baptize with water said to me, "He on whom you see the Spirit descend and remain is the one who baptizes with the Holy Spirit. And I myself have seen and have testified that this is the Son of God.'* (John 1:33-34)

As explained by the Church Fathers Cyril of Jerusalem and John II (4th century Bishop of Jerusalem), the early Judeo-Christians knew three forms of baptism: baptism with water, baptism with fire and baptism with the holy spirit. The baptismal rituals described by John II are reminiscent of the Greco-Roman Mysteries and of primitive initiation rites.

Under the foundations of the Saint-Joseph Church in Nazareth, the French priest Prosper Viaud discovered, in 1908, the remains of a complex carved in the rock, apparently the place where local Judeo-Christians held their baptismal ceremonies. However, only mosaics but no Christian symbols have been found there.

Descending seven stone stairs, the novice entered a subterranean cavern. Probably, it was here that he received the baptism with fire described by John II. The Church Father states that this baptism with fire represented a symbolic 'burning of the old sinful life'.

Afterwards, the novice mounted the same seven stairs and was led to the *baptisterium*. In the corner of the room, he was baptized with water from a basin.

As asserted by Viaud, climbing the seven stairs signified the baptism with the Holy Spirit, through which the novice was promised the eternal life.

Also under the Church of the Annunciation in Nazareth, a similar Judeo-Christian baptistery has been discovered. Graffiti and mural paintings seem to indicate that rituals similar to the Mysteries were performed here, linked to the faith in Jesus Christ, Son of God and Saviour.

It must be noted that graffiti of a clear Christian signature are not found in the deeper and actual baptismal room but on a higher floor. Indeed, when the baptistery of the Church of the Annunciation was discovered, it was completely buried by stones of a local pre-Byzantine sanctuary from before the 5$^{th}$ century. Only these stones had Christian graffiti.

Besides, it is far from certain that the village of Nazareth already existed at the time of Christ! Jesus' surname *the Nazorean* would refer to the *nazoreanship,* a status of sanctity attributed to men and women who lived, since Mosaic times, a very religious life devoted to God. It is not excluded that a pre-Christian Nazorean sect already lived, side by side, in Palestine, with the Pharisees, Sadducees and Essenes.

### Cathars

The 3$^{rd}$ century dualistic sect of the Manicheans affirmed that the central character of the Gospels was known as 'Jesus the Bringer of Light'. The Manicheans rejected the material world. For them, Jesus (not the Son of God, but an Angel from the kingdom of Light) never wore a physical body during his earthly mission, only an 'ether body'.

In the 13th century, the Cathars in the South of France, adopted this Docetic Christology and also preached the dualistic gnosis. For the Cathars, Jesus was not only an angel, but moreover, they claimed that he had been called *Ioannes* in his Divine Kingdom. He would have taken off, or hidden, his light body and had come incognito to the dark Kingdom of the Demiurge (on earth) to preach his salvation doctrine.

The Christian salvation is different from this Gnostic liberation. For the Christian, the baptism is a gift of God, a merciful ritual washing of the Original Sin. The Gnostic, on the other hand, tries through esoteric knowledge, to free his 'personal spirit' from its physical body, in order to transcend a meaningless and poignant earthly existence.

It can be questioned which of these two points of view was actually the one of Jesus.

The Cathars rejected Yahweh's Old Testament and accepted only the Greek canon of the New Testament. They were particularly inspired by the Gospel of John.

Another text to which they referred, was the apocryphal *Ascension of Isaiah*, a visionary Judeo-Christian compilation from the early 2nd century CE. This work focuses on the 'Ascension of Isaiah's Spirit to the Seventh Heaven'. The writer, who identifies himself with the famous prophet of the Old Testament, predicts the future life and sufferings of Jesus Christ, and he receives certain secrets. One of these secrets is about a change in his subtle body, adapted to the celestial plane through which he is travelling.

> '*Such things ye will read and watch ye in the Holy Spirit,*' Isaiah's guardian angel says, '*in order that ye may receive your garments and thrones and crowns of glory, which are laid up in the seventh heaven.*'

**Immortal garment**

The Cathar Perfecti had one central rite, the *Consolamentum* or baptism with the Holy Spirit. This Consolamentum refers to the promised *Parakletos* or Comforter, (bringer of) the Holy Spirit. This very secret baptismal ceremony took place in a room with closed doors and closed windows. In accordance with Acts 8:17, a charismatic laying on of hands would transmit to the rigorously prepared candidate-Perfect the Pauline Spirit gifts.

The Cathars claimed that this seeded the creation of 'heavenly clothes' and in particular of a transcendental Light body. This allowed the reborn 'to see the angels'. At the moment of his physical death, he then could enter lucidly the Light World with his spiritual body.

In the 13th century, the Greek Euthyme wrote:

'*Of those who received the Holy Spirit, it is told* (by the Cathars) *that they do not die, but are transformed, as if sleeping, and that they can effortlessly leave their physical body to cloth themselves with the divine and immortal garment of Christ.*'

These Cathar concepts go back to those of the 3rd century Manicheans, who highly valued the Gnostic *Song of the Pearl*, an Old-Syrian parenthesis in the apocryphal *Acts of Thomas*. In this song, a wandering young man trades a precious pearl that he finds in Egypt for the splendid Garment he once wore in the Kingdom of Heaven (M.R. James, Translation 1924):

'(...) But I remembered not the brightness of it; for I was yet a child and very young when I had left it in the palace of my Father, but suddenly, [when] I saw the garment made like unto me as it had been in a mirror. And I beheld upon it all myself and I knew and saw myself through it, that we were divided asunder, being of one; and again were one in one shape (...) And the likeness of the King of kings was all in all of it. Sapphire stones were fitly set in it above. And again I saw that throughout it motions of knowledge were being sent forth, and it was ready to utter speech. And I heard it speak: I am of him that is more valiant than all men, for whose sake I was reared up with the Father himself. I perceived in myself that my stature grew in accordance with his working. And with its kingly motions it was spreading itself toward me. And it hastened, reaching out from the hand of unto him that would receive it and me also did yearning arouse to start forth and meet it and receive it (...)'
(cf. 2 Corinthians 3:16-18)

### Secret Gospel of Mark

In 1958, the American professor Morton Smith (deceased in 1991), then theology student at Columbia University, discovered in the library of the Orthodox Mar-Saba monastery in Jerusalem, an 18th century copy of an unknown letter of Clement of Alexandria (CE 150-215).

In this letter, Clement mentions to a certain Theodorus the existence of a first – or later adapted – version of the Gospel of Mark, used and falsified by the Gnostic-libertine Karpokratians. The Church Father, as we have seen before, an expert in Platonic philosophy and acquainted with the Eleusinian Mysteries, emphasizes that this Secret Mark was destined for those 'who had made progress in knowledge' and had been initiated into the Great Mysteries.

*'Mark added to his Gospel,'* Clement says, *'a number of sayings, of which he knew that their interpretation would help the initiated mystai to penetrate into the innermost sanctuary of truth hidden by seven veils.'*

Clement cites in his only partially preserved letter to Theodorus, a long and a short paragraph from this unknown Secret Gospel of Mark. He explains that these passages are authentic, but that they do not figure in the canonical Gospel.

The reader will understand right away why the following text (originally in Greek), and particularly Smith's comment on it, aroused the indignation of so many religious Bible exegetes:

*'And they came into Bethany. And a certain woman whose brother had died was there. And, coming, she prostrated herself before Jesus and said to him, "Son of David, have mercy on me". But the disciples rebuked her. And Jesus, being angered, went off with her into the garden where the tomb was, and straightway, going in where the youth was, he stretched forth his hand and raised him, seizing his hand. But the youth, looking upon him, loved him and began to beseech him that he might be with him. And going out of the tomb they came into the house of the youth, for he was rich. And after six days Jesus told him what to do and in the evening the youth came to him, wearing a linen cloth* (sindona) *over his naked body. And he remained with him that night, for Jesus taught him the mystery of the Kingdom of God. And thence, arising, he returned to the other side of the Jordan.'*

To our frustration, Clement's letter to Theodorus stops at the moment when he is on the point of explaining the true significance of the text.

For Morton Smith, who discovered the letter, its content referred to a baptismal ceremony and a (homo) sexually coloured esoteric initiation rite of the earliest Christians. At night and naked. Probably the text alluded to Jesus' baptism with the holy spirit (or baptism with fire?) in view of the resurrection in the Kingdom of God. Smith speculates that during this ceremony, a vision of heavenly spheres was evoked through the monotonous reciting of prayers and hymns.

In the controversial book that Smith later wrote, he suggested that Jesus was a homosexual magician – allegedly Smith's sexual orientation as well – who had learned his consciousness expanding techniques in Egypt. The fact that Jesus would have learned magic tricks in Egypt, had already been mentioned in $2^{nd}$ century rabbinic writings and by the anti-Christian Celsus.

Not all experts consider the Mar-Saba document a reliable copy of the original letter of Clement. Although many historians accept the existence of a Secret Gospel of Mark, they are not so sure about its actual author. As to the significance and veracity of the above-mentioned ritual, the opinions are of course strongly divided.

**Lazarus**
Naturally, the text reminds us of two incidents reported in the canonical Gospels. First of all the raising of Lazarus of Bethany, whose sister addressed Jesus (John 11).

The second canonical passage is an enigmatic, and at first sight irrelevant incident on the Mount of Olives, during the night when Jesus was captured by a hostile crowd (Mark 14:50-53).

*'All of them* (the Apostles) *deserted him* (Jesus) *and fled. A certain young man was following him, wearing nothing but a linen cloth* (sindona). *They caught hold of him, but he left the linen cloth and ran off naked. They took Jesus to the high priest...'*

In John 1:15-16, we learn that Jesus was then followed at a distance by Peter and 'another disciple' who was favorably known by the high priests. This anonymous follower is possibly the one who in the Gospel of John is repeatedly designated as 'the disciple whom Jesus loved' (John 13:23, 19:26, 20:2, 21:20). According to John 21:23, *'the rumor spread in the community that this disciple would not die.'*

It has long been assumed that it was actually this disciple who wrote the Gospel of John. A more recent hypothesis – based on the apocryphal Gospels of Mary and of Philip – claims that the unnamed adherent was none other than Jesus' alleged girlfriend Mary Magdalene!

Miles Fowler and other publicists have recognized in the figure of the 'disciple whom Jesus loved', the reanimated youth of Clement's Secret Gospel of Mark, the regretted and raised friend Lazarus in John 11, the rich young man whom Jesus loved (Mark 10:21), the young man wearing nothing but a linen cloth in Mark 15:51 and finally the young man dressed in a white robe sitting at Jesus' tomb (Mark 16:5).

Intriguing and plausible identifications.

**The Mysteries revisited**
Church Father Clement of Alexandria, formerly Platonist philosopher known as Titus Flavius Clemens, was initiated in the Eleusinian Mysteries. Later converted to Christianity, Clement continued to affirm that not only faith but also *gnosis* (knowledge or understanding) was needed to reach Perfection. The transcendental knowledge he had in mind, was clearly different from the then flourishing Gnostic 'heresies'. In the opinion of Clement, their so called gnosis was just a degenerate form of mysticism.

The Alexandrian Church Father of the late 2$^{nd}$ century coupled the numinous revelations from the original Mysteries to the slowly developing Roman Catholic theology. Clement continued to 'keep the principles of things veiled'. In his digressions on the gnosis, he made a difference between initiates and lay persons.

From his letter to Theodorus, we can deduce that the cited fragment, and probably also other passages in the Secret Gospel of Mark, actually reveal some rites of the Eleusinian Mysteries, recognized as such by the initiated Church Father.

Let us compare the secret procedure in Clement's fragment, and also Jesus' 'union with the Father' and his transfiguration on Mount Tabor, with the following statement of the philosopher Plotinus, which we have already cited:

*'(…) So, to those that approach the Holy Celebrations of the Mysteries, there are appointed purifications and the laying aside of the garments worn before, and the entry in nakedness – until, passing, on the upward way,*

*all that is other than the God. Each in the solitude of himself shall behold that solitary-dwelling Existence, the Apart, the Unmingled, the Pure, that from Which all things depend, for Which all look and live and act and know, the Source of Life and of Intellection and of Being.'*

*'When the spirit sees this divine light, you wonder where it came from: from the inside or the outside world. Then, when it disappears, you say: it was from the inside. And yet, no, it was not from the inside... For in de spiritual world everything dazzles, even he who then beholds it.'*

It is not excluded that Jesus the Nazorean, during his presumed hidden life in Egypt or Syria, had become an adept of a non-Jewish Mystery cult. Yet, it seems to me that his deviating psychobiophysical constitution was more innate, or perhaps the result of a spontaneous Mystery-like experience with far-reaching consequences.

Based on this experience, he later brought his personal message of the Eternal Life.

*'I am the resurrection and the life. Those who believe in me, even though they die, will live, and everyone who lives and believes in me will never die.'*

And he created his own initiation rite (the baptism with the Holy Spirit/Fire).

'The exclusive character of the enterprise is remarkable: both Jesus and the antique Mysteries emphasized that only the initiate could expect the blissful eternal life. This is, by the way, the conviction of Chinese Taoists as well.

Despite Paul's formulation that 'Christ had openly shown the *mysterion*', even Jesus remained cautious in his words: only those who 'had ears to hear' would receive the mysteries of God's Kingdom. The populace had to be satisfied with moral admonitions and parables (Mark 4:34).

## Baptism with fire

Even though there is a consistent link between the Mysteries, the words and actions of Jesus, and the resurrection doctrine of Paul, we are left with the person of Jesus as a 'miracle worker'. An initiation may (as in the near-death experience) convince a mystes of an afterlife, yet it does not enable him to reanimate a dead body!

A number of passages in the Gospels suggest that Jesus was capable to achieve the mystical Union described by Plotinus. Apparently he had free access to the spiritual Light, to which I have already repeatedly referred, – and which according to John 1:4 equals Life – and made use of it when needed.

It must have been this capacity that he had in mind, when he said following his startling healing of a cripple at the pool of Beth-Zatha:

*'My Father is still working, and I also am working.'* (John 5:17)

Although the evangelical baptism with fire is often considered to be the same as the baptism with the Holy Spirit, this is probably not correct. From Luke 12:49, 50 we learn indeed that the baptism with fire was directly related to the death- and resurrection process:

*'I came to bring fire to the earth, and how I wish it were already kindled! I have a baptism with which to be baptized, and what stress I am under until it is completed!'*

Jesus, apparently to a certain extent clairvoyant in space and time, not only predicted many times his future sufferings, but also his own resurrection. It looks as if the confidence in his clairvoyance and sublime power was so strong, that he even thought he could resuscitate his own dead body!

*'You do not know what you are asking,'* he replied defiantly to James and John, who requested him for a good place in God's Kingdom. *'Are you able to drink the cup that I drink, or be baptized with the baptism that I am baptized with?'* (Mark 10:38)

For John 10:17-18 there is no doubt that Jesus, at least at that moment, was sure of his case:

*'For this reason the Father loves me, because I lay down my life in order to take it up again. No one takes it from me, but I lay it down of my own accord. I have power to lay it down, and I have power to take it up again. I have received this command from my Father.'*

Is it possible that this idea of resurrection gradually became an *idée-fixe* or obsession for him? Because on other occasions, Jesus also expressed his all too human fears and doubts:

*'Now my soul is troubled. And what should I say — "Father, save me from this hour"? No, it is for this reason that I have come to this hour.'* (John 12:27)

Shortly before he is arrested on the Mount of Olives, a terrified Jesus sweats 'drops of blood'. And on the cross, physically and mentally totally exhausted, he realizes to his dismay that he, after all, may have been mistaken:

*'Eli Eli lama sabachtani?',* which according to Mark translates as *'My God, my God, why have you forsaken me?'* (cf. Psalm 22:1)

Interestingly, in the apocryphal Gospel of Peter is written:

*'My force, my force, why have you left me?'*

The Hebrew word *El* can indeed be translated into Greek as *dynamin* (force, power) or as *Theo* (God)…

Even though it was written later than the canonical Gospels, the liberal theologian John Crossan thinks that this Gospel of Peter actually refers to older sources.

## Rebirth

As the Sabbath was approaching, the Jewish Council asked Pilate to break the legs of the three crucified victims, in order to hasten their death and the removal of their bodies from the place of execution. Jesus' legs were exceptionally not smashed, as he was – according to the Gospel of John – already dead. A Roman soldier pierced Jesus' side with a spear *'and at once there came out blood and water'*.

This unusual practice raises some questions.

Besides some pious women and the Apostle John, two prominent and fortunate Pharisees were also present at the execution: Joseph of Arimathea 'honourable member of the Council' and Nicodemus 'a leader of the Jews'. John's Gospel explains that both men had become disciples of Jesus, albeit in secret, fearing expulsion by the Jewish community.

Pilate allowed Joseph of Arimathea to remove Jesus' body. A permission rarely granted, but it protected the body from its usual fate: food for the vultures. Nicodemus brought a mixture of myrrh and aloe, weighing one hundred Roman pound – more than 30 kilo! – of medicinal herbs preventing putrefaction.

The evangelist continues:

*'They took the body of Jesus and wrapped it with the spices in linen cloths, according to the burial custom of the Jews. Now there was a garden in the place where he was crucified, and in the garden there was a new tomb in which no one had ever been laid.'* (John 19:40, 41)

Very intriguing, this touching interest of Jesus' secret disciples! Especially when one knows that Nicodemus, on one occasion, had a nightly conversation with Jesus about the 'rebirth' (the *Jewish Encyclopedia* states that this prominent disciple could be no other than the Talmudic Nicodemus ben Gorion, a Jewish Saint, also famous as a miracle worker!)

'How can a man be born when he is old?' a surprised Nicodemus asked on that occasion. The prominent member of the Sanhedrin must have understood by then that Jesus was talking about something else than just the baptism with water.

And so Jesus declared:

*'Very truly, I tell you, no one can see the Kingdom of God without being born from above (…) I tell you, no one can enter the Kingdom of God without being born of water and Spirit. What is born of the flesh is flesh, and what is born of the Spirit is spirit. Do not be astonished that I said to you, "You must be born from above". The wind* (pneuma) *blows where it chooses, and you hear the sound of it, but you do not know where it comes from or where it goes. So it is with everyone who is born of the Spirit* (pneuma)' (John 3: 3, 5-8)

The four Gospels gloriously end with an extraordinary feat of strength. Was the physical resurrection of Jesus' body needed to give a visible evidence that his teachings of the 'spiritual rebirth' had been more than just the boasting of a big mouth?

# VI

# THE LIGHT BODY

Let us now go back to the exceptional mental and physiological properties of Jesus the Nazorean, and the unusual faculties that may have enabled him to leave his alleged imprint on the Turin Shroud.

By birth or as the result of a 'spiritual rebirth' – in circumstances that we only can guess – Jesus had a number of unique abilities. The most remarkable ones were related to 'force' and 'light', two electromagnetic phenomena. Let us see to what extent Jesus' specific force and specific light have something to do with physical phenomena known in biology and physics.

In his seminal work *Vehicles of Consciousness (Ochèma, History and Meaning of Hylic Pluralism),* the Dutch philosopher J.J. Poortman gave a detailed discussion of the belief that there exist body-forms, composed of a more subtle substance than a mere organic one. To make his point, Poortman collected testimonies and conceptions from all over the world, and from different cultures.

There is, for instance, the so called ghost body, an astral, etheric, or eventual separation body. As is the case for the biological body, such a meta-organism is frequently described in the mystical literature as a 'vehicle' or a 'cloth'. It is usually invisible, and it can offer an explanation for paranormal phenomena such as telekinesis, out-of-body experiences and near-death experiences.

Poortman could identify at least three kinds of subtle bodies. He classified them as follows:

1. The *physiological* pneuma (Greek: spirit, here 'fine matter'): which is probably called by H.P. Blavatsky the etheric double. For Poortman its activity is based on a sort of electromagnetic waves or radiation.
2. The *psychic* pneuma, driven by a hypothetical psychic energy. Probably the astral or mental body of the Theosophical literature.
3. The *sublime* pneuma or luminous body. Related to the resurrection concept of the New Testament and to the well-known light phenomena documented, time and again, in religious and mystical literature.

Angels always appear as shining figures; in the Bible they are often referred to with the words *ruah* and *pneuma*.

In the Christian, but also in the Taoist and Tibetan iconography, the head of sacred figures is surrounded by a golden aura.

Parapsychologist W.H.C. Tenhaeff noticed that *'through the ages, the apparitions of the dying and deceased have been described as radiating and shining shapes (...) Sometimes the apparition is preceded by a light flash (...) In different cultures, the afterlife is represented as the Land of Light. The inhabitants of this Land are represented as Light figures.'*

**Body of fire**
Similarities with the resurrection- or transfiguration body of Jesus are found in numerous texts of the mystical world literature.

The esoteric/magical tracts of the *Corpus Hermeticum* of the 2nd century CE speak of an 'immortal body, the body of fire'.

The, already mentioned, Old-Chinese meditation manual *The Secret of the Golden Flower* describes a technique to make a new, immortal light-, breath- or diamond-body.

In the Old-Hinduistic *Laws of Manu* one can read of a pious person who eventually reaches the 'heavenly light world', clothed with a spiritual form.

The physical body of an illuminated Dzogchen-practitioner (Tibetan Buddhism) transforms at the moment of his death in a Rainbow-Body.

The Neoplatonists of the 3rd century CE call it *to augoeidès ochèma* or 'the radiating body'. Their Gnostic contemporaries speak of a 'garment of light', and the 13th century Cathars of a 'light body' that has to be regained.

The final aim of transcendental magic (*theurgy* for the Neoplatonists) is to create an astral and autonomous spiritual- or light body, in which the self-consciousness can be transferred, so as to enable a final separation from the physical body. By doing so, the theurg can lever the barrier between the earthly sphere and the lower and higher spiritual spheres, thus avoid the sleep of death.

The light-body is, almost certainly, also the elaborated theme of the *Chymical Wedding,* attributed to Christian Rosencreutz. This German manifesto (1459) tells about an alchemistically resuscitated royal couple that, as stated by the founder of the legendary Rosicrucian Order, receives *'curious white garments the like of which I had never seen in the castle, nor can I describe them, for I thought that they were nothing other than crystal; but they were soft, and not transparent; so that I cannot describe them...'*

In the opinion of the Anthroposophists, these white, royal garments refer to the subtle etheric body. The Austrian visionary Rudolf Steiner ascertained that Christian Rosencreutz must have had such an indestructible etheric body himself.

*'Which means,'* the anthroposophically oriented author Bastiaan Baan writes in his comments on the Chymical Wedding, *'that he can always be connected – be it alive or dead – with his companions on earth.'*

A tractate of the 18th century declares *'that the whole process of the philosophical work is about dividing and hardening; i.e. the dissolution of the body and the hardening of the spirit.'*

It is interesting to note that the alchemistic procedures and even the vocabulary of the *Chymical Wedding* and of the Chinese *Golden Flower* are remarkably similar.

**Laser therapy**

The sublime pneuma or radiating body (see Poortman) has powerful (re)generating properties. It must be this sublime pneuma that Jesus emanated during his miraculous healings and resuscitations of the dead, and that also activated his own resurrection body.

For skeptics, all this must sound very dubious. Nevertheless, it is possible to put such a vitalising (light) force in a more or less rational context. There is indeed, in modern biophysics, a phenomenon that can be connected with this radiating pneuma.

In the twenties of the previous century, the Russian biologist and embryologist Alexander Gurwitsch demonstrated that two plants, separated by a quartz glass plate, showed some form of communication between them. The cells of a rooting onion appeared to send out light signals to the onion on the other side of the plate, so that the latter started to root in the direction of the former.

Subsequently, it was discovered that living cells thus emit not only biochemical messages, but also very weak electromagnetic signals. Diseased cells influence healthy ones and *vice versa*, by means of genuine light waves between the ultraviolet and the infrared.

From this originated the laser therapy. Tissue fibroblasts and macrophages (eliminating non-self and dead cells) can be stimulated by red and infrared laser light. Poorly healing wounds can be cured more quickly by this laser treatment.

Thus, directed and dosed electric currents (without dehydrating heat) can promote the growth and repair of living tissue.

A publication in the British journal *Nature* described, in 2006, the first genes and their encoded proteins, that promote the movement of cells and the wound repair, induced by this ultra-weak electrical current.

## St. Elmo's fire

Our body is under the continuous influence of positively and negatively charged atmospheric particles. The beneficial effect of negatively charged ions is now generally accepted. Ionized air increases the oxygen content of the blood and improves the hormonal system and cellular metabolism. This type of electrically charged particles is found in large concentrations in nature: near waterfalls, at the seaside and in the mountains.

It is remarkable how often the Gospels mention an exhausted Jesus who retires into the mountains (to 'recharge his battery'?). And it is probably not fortuitous that the transfiguration of Jesus took place on a mountain (compare Moses' transfiguration on Mount Sinai).

Automatically comes to mind the famous St. Elmo's fire, the coronal discharge from sharp objects during a thunderstorm.

*'Farmers can be confronted with a "sea of cold prickling fire" and feel as if their hands or moustache are on fire,'* I read in a paper on the internet from Danny Caes, an expert in optic-atmospheric phenomena (Ghent University Public Observatory).

St. Elmo's fire is reported especially by mountain climbers. Harmless as such, but announcing a serious and hefty sound-and-light show. The increased ionization of oxygen molecules in a cloud and an amplified electrical field on the ground create a voltage differential that results in the coronal discharge.

Danny Caes also reported on mysterious sounds during electromagnetic and geophysical disturbances: bangs, cracks, rumbling, sputtering and/or hissing.

Mark's Gospel mentions explicitly a cloud that was overshadowing Jesus on Mount Tabor. It is possible that Jesus' transfiguration light was actually the result of an interaction between an electromagnetic effect and his 'powerful' biophysical constitution. Conceivably, the Nazorean had already experienced this effect on his body during his lonely mountain walks, and now wanted to astound his disciples with it.

The enigmatic explanation in the apocryphal Gospel of the Hebrews, of which only fragments are conserved, possibly refers to this:

*'And my mother, the Holy Spirit, took me by one hair and led me to the great mountain Tabor.'*

A remarkable story in the Belgian weekly woman magazine *Libelle* (April 1995), fits perfectly well with our subject. A certain Marlene (42) told reporter Elle Vermeulen the poignant history of how she was struck by lightning on the beach, two years earlier. As by wonder, Marlene escaped from death:

*'(…) How long I have sat there, I do not remember. My watch had stopped. When I closed my hands to rub off the sand, two blue sparks flew of (…) My whole body tingled and prickled, all my clothes were cracking (…) Back in the car, I cried for a while. Each time when I touched the steering wheel or my keys, I got a shock. Afterwards, when I started the car, the motor stopped after a few seconds (…) But worst of all were the flashes that I saw in my head. They lasted for two, three seconds and I saw things that I had preferred not seeing. Things that were shown on the television news three days later (…)'*

**Human Batteries**

This brings us to a very unusual phenomenon, hardly known to most people.

The nervous system works by means of electrochemical signals. A very weak electromagnetic field surrounds our brain, field that produces brain waves that can be measured by electroencephalography (EEG). Sometimes, this electric energy, for one reason or another, becomes so strong that it 'escapes' and starts to influence objects outside the body (with or without direct contact). Human Batteries, disputed in scientific circles, actually represent an extreme form of this phenomenon.

Many of us have had the unpleasant experience of receiving a small shock when closing the car's door after getting out of the vehicle. Friction against the car seat has caused in the body a temporal imbalance of electric charges (static electricity). With the disagreeable effect of an electrical discharge when the metallic car door is touched.

Human Batteries are thought to constantly carry such a powerful and unstable electromagnetic field within them. Apparently the charge seems to increase under emotional stress and sometimes the consequences are very nasty.

Human Batteries experience electric discharges all day long. Often brief sparks leap from their fingertips, when they unintentionally touch other persons or when they open doors, closets, drawers or when they pick up an object.

Completely crazy is the SLI phenomenon (Street Light Interference). As the word indicates, this happens when Human Batteries disturb, unwillingly, street and traffic lights. Occasionally, the lighting of an entire street is affected!

Every once in a while, these persons cause trouble in computers, radios, television sets, magnetrons, dashboards etc. Some report of fading light traces when drawing lines in the sand. A genuine curiosity cabinet of electric incidents!

Of course, Human Batteries are not so happy with their 'talent'. There exist even specialized internet sites where these *'weirdos'* can find help for their misunderstood and critically received problem. At first sight, this is horror writer Stephen King at his best. Nevertheless, the countless, often desperate, testimonies make one frown the eyebrows.

Particularly intriguing are the Human Batteries who – as Marlene did – mention extrasensory perception in space and time. This apparently is an occasional side effect of their exceptional constitution. Most Human Batteries suffered from an electric shock in their childhood or were once – as the Belgian woman Marlene – struck by lightning.

The must see website *The weird science database of Electric People* states that, when emotions tend to become too strong (and when their 'electric charge' and its accompanying hindrance increase significantly), Human Batteries can alleviate their problem by respiratory control and meditation.

The following testimony is of special interest because of its mention of 'fiery tongues' and the well-known white light. A woman reported to feel 'strange' during her household activities:

*'I have to sit down... Then I see a clear light flash coming from somewhere deep in my brain. Then I send forth literally an incredible painful spark. I smell the odour of an electric fire. On two occasions, other persons have witnessed these phenomena.'*

In his book *Poltergeist!* (1981), the British writer Colin Wilson points to the fact that the centre of such 'spiritualistic disturbances' is often a telekinetically gifted Human Battery. Wilson and other researchers have argued that Human Batteries are 'fed' bio-energetically, for an undetermined period of time, by electromagnetic earth forces...

## Spontaneous human combustion

The so called *Spontaneous human combustion* (SHC) is another phenomenon classified by skeptics as twaddle. The fact that a human body, all of a sudden and without an external cause, catches fire and is incinerated in a very short time, is indeed hard to reconcile with known physical and biological processes. As specified by one theory, SHC is caused by a rare electrochemical reaction in the body of an overheated 'Human Battery'.

Here is a creepy and weird example that illustrates how eccentric the phenomenon can be. The case was reported by Larry E. Arnold in his amazing book *Ablaze!* (1995).

On the early morning of September 13th, 1967, passengers in Auckland Street, south London, suddenly see a strong flash behind the windows of an abandoned house. Someone calls the fire brigade and five minutes later, Commander John Stacey and his team are on the spot.

When they get in, the surprised firemen find a burning body at the bottom of the stairs. It is the body of Robert Bailey, a notorious alcoholic, who had looked for shelter the previous night.

*'He was half turned on his right side,'* Commander Stacy subsequently testified, *'with his knees folded to his body, as if he wanted to suppress the pain in his abdomen. From what appeared to be a cut wound of about 10 cm, a blue flame was gushing out under high pressure, as if it were some sort of gas burner.'*

They needed a couple of fire extinguishers to control the fire. Bailey's clothes were only scorched on his belly and there was a burned hole in the plank floor where his body had lain.

The poor man – who had clenched himself with his teeth into the newel post! – died shortly afterwards. Initially, the coroner Gavin Thurston wanted to classify the case as 'death from asphyxiation caused by fire smoke'. A second investigation concluded 'cause of death unknown'.

Who will say that the following words of the 11th century mystic Symeon the New Theologian (more about him in Chapter VIII) are inappropriate here?

*'If a man carries in him the light of the Holy Spirit but cannot resist its radiance, he will fall down and scream from fear and dismay, as someone who experiences something supernatural, beyond all words and reason. He will be as a man of whom the intestines are on fire and, not capable to endure the scorched flame, he will be destroyed by it...'*

Might there be a connection between Simeon's 'light of the Holy Spirit' and what the Old Indian sacral text Rig-Veda describes as *tapas*? Tapas stands for the 'internal heat' that a yogi can generate and control within himself, through specific breathing techniques. This tapas activates in the yogi miraculous skills such as clairvoyance, levitation, and making oneself invisible…

**Biological plasma body**
In the thirties of the last century, two Armenian electrical engineers, Semyon and Valentina Kirlian, developed the Kirlian photography. An organic object placed on a photographic plate connected to a high-voltage source, was found to produce a remarkable image, similar to a coronal discharge. A sort of aura of coloured flashes, sparks and rays was observed, surrounding, for instance, the leaf of a tree or a fingertip.

In 1968, biochemists and biophysicists of the Kazakh Kirov State University in Alma-Ata postulated that this phenomenon was the reflection of a biological plasma body. They proposed that the very mobile, gaseous halo (which since then has also been recorded on film) was composed of positive ions and free electrons, i.e. from plasma, the fourth aggregation state of matter. The Kirlians had previously postulated that the high-voltage field they used in their photography, converted a non-electromagnetic bioplasmic phenomenon into a visible electromagnetic one.

Curiously, a leaf from which a part had been cut, still showed on the Kirlian photo an aura of the intact leaf. Did this have something to do with the so called phantom pains and ghost limbs, described by patients who previously underwent an amputation? A question that can be easily answered with the etheric double model, but which sounds as a curse in the context of the current neuroscientific paradigm (nowadays, the dissident cell biologist Rupert Sheldrake is one of the few scientists, who still make the link between phantom pains and a subtle body).

The biological plasma body, discovered by the Russians (and which was received rather sceptically in the West), apparently had an organized structure. It seemed to be revitalized regularly by... the respiration. Analysis of the different colours was said to be of help in predicting and diagnosing latent diseases. Moreover, adding ionized air to unbalanced plasma could speed up the healing process.

Significant in the perspective of the central thesis in this book (fully explained in Chapter VIII and IX), are the experiments showing a link between the healing 'laying on of hands' and an increase in the plasma body energy. Excitement, expressions of willpower and also successful telepathic and telekinetic experiments could increase the typical activity of the bioplasmic corona. The faintly shining corona of self-declared *psychics* (as, to a certain extent, Jesus also must have been) showed a remarkable bluish glow when they went into trance.

Later, Thelma Moss and Ken Johnson of the University of California repeated these photographic experiments in a high-voltage field. With similar results.

In the scientific world, Kirlian's bioplasma and the so called bio-energetic field or biofield remain highly controversial. Skeptics state that the 'technological indications' are only optical, photographic and electromagnetic side effects of organic electromagnetic processes.

Of course, some caution is certainly needed: in that period of Russian history, many pseudo-scientists were scientifically endorsed and sanctioned by the Soviet regime.

**Metamorphosis**
Is there a connection between this hypothetical plasma body or biofield and the sublime pneuma mentioned by J.J. Poortman, the pneumatic body the Apostle Paul talks about, and the glorified body of Jesus the Nazorean?

The New Testament speaks of transfiguration, transformation, metamorphosis. Was it actually a powerful discharge of Jesus' bioplasma body, resulting in the spectacular biophysical light effect?

What if this metamorphosis had something to do with an abrupt nuclear fission, liberating a stream of protons and neutrons? But then again, the question remains how a physical body could trigger such a process that nowadays can only be realized in a particle accelerator. Unless one has to do with naturally decaying isotopes.

It is known that radioactive radiation can darken a photographic plate. The leaf of a plant fed on radioactive phosphorus 32, leaves on the plate a detailed black imprint.

Plants conserved between two pages of a book can sometimes leave remarkably detailed negative imprints on the paper. Nobody has an explanation for this. Moreover, one cannot predict whether it will happen or not. An imprint, however, will only be formed before the plant has withered.

In 1937, Prof. J. Volckringer of the Université de Paris made a connection between this process and the imprint on the Turin Shroud. By chance he had found in an old book the perfect negative image of a plant of the genus *Scrophularia* (figwort).

The Flemish chemist Remi Van Haelst writes in his study *Het Gelaat van Kristus* (The Face of Christ) how, in 1982, NASA-expert John da Silvo had the Scrophularia imprint analysed in a VP8 Image Analyzer: a three-dimensional image was obtained, exactly of the same quality as that of the 3D image of the man on the Turin linen.

**Bioluminescence**

The Transfiguration Light is also reminiscent of a phenomenon called biological light or *bioluminescence*.

A number of organisms spontaneously produce light: bacteria, fungi, algae, insects, worms, fishes and some crustaceans. Everybody knows the fire fly or the remarkable deep-sea fishes with their light lanterns. Some insects emit light at regular short intervals. This light may play a role in reproduction rituals, to keep an enemy at a distance or to catch a prey. The function is not always known.

The American biochemists William D. McElroy and Howard H. Seliger explain that bioluminescence may have offered a specific advantage to certain species. There was a time, when the atmosphere was still devoid of oxygen. A lot of primitive organisms became extinct when oxygen concentration increased (as the result of plant photosynthesis). Other creatures could survive by converting the oxygen into new chemical compounds. The energy liberated in these organisms was in the form of light, not harmful heat. This light is called 'cold light', in contrast to light accompanied by heat. Research on luminescent organisms has shown that the light is produced by a biochemical oxidation process (interaction with oxygen) which involves specific enzymes. A chain reaction results in the formation of an oxygenated substrate (a light-emitting pigment).

Like all birds and like the other mammals, man is a species that has developed a metabolism that is entirely dependent on oxygen.

Especially in Russia, scientific publications have reported on spontaneous bioluminescent discharges by living organisms, which are very weak (and difficult to detect in humans). This spontaneous bioluminescence is likewise the result of a biochemical reaction, similar to the production of electrically charged molecules (for example, reactive oxygen and nitrogen intermediates) by immune cells, more in particular macrophages.

Some contemporary, more or less vitalist scientists – for instance the American biophysicist Dr Beverly Rubik – do not exclude the possibility that these *biophotons* (light particles of biological origin) and electrically charged biomolecules have a regulating function in nerve and other cells of the human body (Biophotons from the 'human biofield' have actually been measured and visualized with different detectors.)

In 1923, the (already mentioned) Russian biologist Alexander Gurwitsch speculated that dividing cells emit ultraviolet light to stimulate neighbouring cells to do the same.

The origin of the ultraviolet components in the *ultra-weak-bioluminescence* (UWB) is not elucidated for the moment. Refinement of detection methods for UWB may in the future help with medical diagnosis (and perhaps detection of tumour cells). The measurement of UWB at the fingertips has already been correlated with different pathological and physiological conditions and with the ageing process.

**Anna Monaro**

In his excellent study *The Physical Phenomena of Mysticism*, Herbert Thurston s.j. dedicates an entire chapter to mystical light phenomena. This British Jesuit and physician examined the relationship between extreme devotion and luminous manifestations that sometimes accompany it. In the conclusion of his book, he expresses his confusion with respect to the similarities of the light phenomena with some spiritualistic manifestations (despised by him).

An example that fits with our subject is the case of 'the luminous or glowing woman'.

In May 1934, Anna Monaro, suffering from severe asthma, was admitted to the hospital in Pirano, Italy. The doctors were surprised to see that a brief, bluish glow radiated periodically from the breast of the sleeping woman. The phenomenon lasted for weeks.

The physician in charge Giocondo Protti used a film camera to capture the precise nature and duration of this phenomenon.

In a lecture he gave at Padua University, Protti explained that it concerned *'a profound change in the neurovegetative system as a result of compulsive religious thoughts and by austere fasting.'*

During the light discharges, the respiration and heart frequency of Signora Monaro increased alarmingly, resulting in a profuse perspiration. Dr Protti has argued that the organism of the woman produced during her fasting *'a strong discharge of sulphur-containing compounds, which was stimulated by an abnormally high concentration of ultraviolet properties in her blood.'* [sic]

**Saints of fire**

Light phenomena are frequently reported in hagiographies (biographies of saints). The following citation of the learned Archbishop Prospero Lambertini from his unusually critical calendar of Saints *De Beatificatione et Canonisatione* (1743) was also recorded by Thurston.

Having heard and read numerous testimonies, Lambertini, the later humanistic and enlightened Pope Benedict XIV, declares:

*'... it seems to be a well-recognized fact: sometimes visible flames surround a human body and the whole persona can radiate with a natural fire. Not as flames that flare up, but more like sparks that jump from all sides. Moreover, some saints glow with a burning light that does not come from within them, but from their cloths, scepter or sword they carry.'*

Everyday electromagnetic inducers of the phenomenon (sort of St. Elmo's fire) cannot always be excluded; certainly not if, as in the latter case, a scepter or sword is mentioned.

But how about the following incident?

During the sanctification process of the Italian mystic Bernardino Realino in 1621, the nobleman Tobias da Ponte made this amazing declaration. One day, while visiting the pious priest, he had to wait before the door of his cell. Da Ponte sat for some time on a chair in the corridor. Suddenly he noticed the door was ajar and through it he perceived an odd, bright light. Alarmed, the nobleman pushed open the door and saw to his surprise the radiant priest as if kneeling, but floating above the floor at about half a meter. Da Ponte was so scared that he immediately ran home.

Other people occasionally had seen sparks, as fiery tongues, flow out of Realino's body *('scintillava da tutto il corpo come scintille di fuoco')*.

Some of these phenomena were also reported for the French visionary Bernadette Soubirous. Witnesses declared that they once saw the asthmatic girl running in a meadow without touching the ground. An aunt with whom Bernadette stayed, one night found the sleeping girl bathing in a glowing white light.

Bernadette Soubirous died in 1879 of tuberculosis of the bones. Her body was exhumed in 1909, 1919 and 1923 (the first time on the occasion of her canonization process). Three times the sworn members of the committee declared that her remains were odourless and hardly showed signs of decay.

Today, Bernadette's body (still relatively intact, with hands and face protected by a wax coating) is displayed in a transparent coffin in the monastery chapel of Nevers.

Also the bodies of the Parisian visionary Catherine Labouré, the Portuguese girl Jacinta of Fatima, and the Belgian visionary Leonie van den Dijck, (as well as those of about ten other Catholic and Orthodox saints), were found to be largely intact after exhumation.

Of course, skeptics classify all this as selective observation, pious exaggeration and the effect of natural processes. Still, I wonder whether there is a link between those mystics, of whom the body remained intact long after their death, and the ones who experienced luminous sensations during their lifetime.

Particularly curious is the case of the very pious Saint Charbel Makhlouf (1828-1898) from the Lebanese Maronite Order (part of the Eastern Catholic Churches). After the death and interment of this holy hermit, bright lights were perceived for weeks above his grave in Annaya cemetery. The superiors of the Monastery of St. Maron opened the tomb to find Makhloufs body still fresh. Since then, a rosy, bloodlike liquid flows from it. University doctors could not explain the enduring generation of the oil- or sweatlike substance, and the persistent flexibility and incorruptibility of the corpse. When Makhlouf was unearthed for a third and fourth time in 1950 and 1952 – over half a century later! – his supple body still was relatively intact.

Of the sickly saint Lidwina of Schiedam, her famous biographer Thomas A. Kempis wrote:
> *Although she stayed most of the time in the dark and could not tolerate the sunlight, she was elated*

*about the divine light: witnesses saw that sometimes at night her little cell was so brightly lit, as if lamps or a fire had been ignited. We do not have to be surprised that even her body irradiated with the divine light, as also the apostle Saint Paul saw with unveiled face the Glory of the Lord, and who day after day changed in the same image, from light to light, as with the Spirit of the Lord (2 Corinthians 3:18).'*

Another example are the testimonies of the increased body temperature of the Italian Padre Pio (Francesco Forgione, 1887-1968), when he was in a trance. The body of this well-known (and likewise asthmatic) friar of the Minor Capuchin order, would really be hot at these moments. When celebrating the Eucharist, the stigmatized priest was so entranced that bystanders reported they saw his face really glowing. Padre Pio called this a 'fiery feeling'.

In a secular context, the phenomenon of light is associated especially with the near-death experience. Melvin Morse, the American pediatrician who became famous – and later became controversial – for his NDE- research on reanimated children, wrote in the *American Journal of Diseases of Children:*
'One way or the other, there was always light.'

A panicking father dived twelve meter deep to save his drowning daughter. He found her because she was glowing: she bathed in a bubble of white light...

Eleven-year-old Joe, reported to be clinically dead, saw his body from a bird's eye view lying, surrounded by a soft white light.

*'I heard a sizzling sound,'* the reanimated boy later told, *'and instantly I was squatting against a corner of the ceiling. I saw my body down below, emitting light as if I had a light bulb in me…'*

## Stigmata

No doubt, Padre Pio, Capuchin friar of San Giovanni Rotonda, will be mostly remembered for his stigmata. For fifty years, until he died in 1968, he was continually confronted with his bleeding palms.

Is there a connection with the blood stains on the Turin Shroud?

Not excluded…

The most famous stigmatized person in history is certainly the much-honoured Francis of Assisi (1186-1226). Among the more than three hundred other persons, who were reported to have bleedings in locations corresponding to the crucifixion wounds of Jesus, the best known are Catharina of Sienna, Teresa of Avila, Rita of Cascia and more recently the visionaries Catherine Emmerich, Therese Neumann and the Belgian Louise Lateau.

Lateau (1850-1883) was examined in detail by members of the Belgian Royal Academy of Medicine in 1874. Doctor Lefebvre of Leuven University performed experiments with sealed gloves and socks (later even with a closed glass tube).

Conclusion: no fraud, as maintained by Lefebvre, the wounds and spontaneous bleedings were real, but they could not be rationally explained.

Comparative research led to a couple of astonishing observations. The majority of the stigmatized lived in

Italy and were member of a Catholic order. The phenomenon was reported seven times more frequently in women than in men. Some showed the stigmata at the early age of nine, others had passed the age of seventy.

Different from case to case, the most perfect ones showed simultaneously all the bleeding signs of the Passion. Also, they often appeared on, for Christians significant, Friday. On both hands and feet, in the flank (most frequently left) and as point-shaped wounds on the head (thorn crown).

'Sweat' and 'tears' of blood also occured. In rare cases, the hands and feet showed bulges of the skin, in the form of actual nails.

All this is accompanied by intense pain and often associated with the most eccentric ailments. The stigmatic is frequently the center of similar paranormal phenomena: the well-known harassment by poltergeists, a perfumed smell of flowers, bilocation (the physical body seen in two places at the same time), defying gravity and unusually long fasting.

Furthermore, there are the many fabulous stories of 'levitating wafers' and 'celebrating the Eucharist at distance'.

Of course, for all these side phenomena, we have to rely on the testimonies of the concerned persons and the devout witnesses.

During his or her almost continuous state of ecstasy, the stigmatic shows signs of complete mental isolation. The pulse and respiration are slowed down. The facial expression is unnaturally intense. Occasionally, moving lips betray a conversation with an invisible presence.

The stigmatic regularly comments on dramatic visions of Catholic signature: reliving and sometimes interacting with the Passion story. Presumably, the mysterious and often documented 'state of contemplative rest' is closely related to these religious visions. And probably to the mentioned paranormal phenomena as well.

**Hysteria?**

A Divine grace for most Catholic believers, yet certainly not a compelling article of faith. The freethinking skeptic is confronted with the declarations of authenticity by many experienced physicians. What then could account for all this?

A side effect of a hysteric neurosis is the most frequent explanation. In the professional literature on cognitive psychology, all sorts of spontaneous and suggested bleedings and swellings of the skin have indeed been reported, independent of a religious context.

At the end of the 19th century, the ultra-Catholic French Doctor Antoine Imbert-Gourbeyre attempted to defend the cases of stigmatization against the rationalization by the Parisian *Ecole de la Salpêtrière* with two fist-thick vindications. His opponents were the renowned neurologists Charcot and Janet.

The psychiatric literature speaks of psychosomatic afflictions, of a pathological propensity to be influenced, of bleedings 'on order' and of physiological reactions to hypnotic suggestion.

It is a fact that stigmatization often resembles the spontaneous and equally significant physical symptoms of hysteria. Although in the case of stigmatization, the famous eccentricity of the hysteric 'conversion' is highly emphatic.

All stigmatics have in common to be extremely religious. Psychoanalysts explain the stigmata as the expression of subconscious religious fears or desires (perhaps somewhat surprisingly, even the well-informed Jesuit H. Thurston speaks of 'devout obsession' and of a 'crucification complex').

Of course, all this does not refute the reality and the paranormal nature of the stigmata phenomena. Especially when one has to conclude that they are often accompanied by other bizarre phenomena of a parapsychic and paraphysical nature.

All seems to indicate that a mental disorder (psychoneurosis, psychosis or, for instance, the effect of a psychedelic drug or of excessive asceticism) can indeed 'expand' the action radius and receptivity of the personal consciousness. Albeit generally in an uncontrolled fashion and often accompanied by immense fear and suffering.

From this pried-open psychic source, extreme mental aberrations may come to the surface. However, a causal relationship between abstract ideas and – occasionally very specific and localized – corresponding physical reactions, cannot be scientifically demonstrated. Not to mention the eventual (para)physical repercussions in the surroundings of the concerned person.

In even rarer cases, the stigmatized body presents the specific, well-known 'mystical' properties.

# VII

# KUNDALINI

According to an old tradition, Jesus made arduous journeys to India and Tibet before his public appearance and/or after his resurrection in Judea. Some have heard in Jesus' teachings the echoes of Vedic or Buddhist doctrines (cf. *The Unknown Life of Jesus Christ* by the Russian journalist Nicolos Notowitch, 1894.)

Even if an actual trip to India is far from certain, there are undoubtedly connections between the light phenomena reported around Jesus' persona, the imprint on the Turin Shroud, and the exotic subject I will discuss in this chapter.

An Old Indian spiritual doctrine teaches that there slumbers a fiery force or energy in the human body. Like a sleeping snake, this force (Kundalini) lays coiled at the base of the spine. There is an extensive Hindu literature on this subject, particularly in texts that deal with the so called Tantric yoga. Kundalini yoga focuses especially on sexual impulses. Besides its role in procreation, the sexual drive can be a potent way to spiritual self-development.

As maintained by the Tantric doctrine, the physical body has seven centers of force or *chakras*. They are a sort of turning wheels, whirling and colourful when fully 'awake', yet invisible to the physical eye, because embedded in the etheric human double. These subtle force centers are arranged in a column along the spinal cord, connected by vertical channels. Their role is to attract subtle energies that feed the corresponding glands and nerve centers. The best known are the root, heart, throat and crown chakra.

The Kundalini slumbers in the root chakra *(muladhara)*. Appropriate mystical techniques can awaken the Kundalini force. What ensues is a radical reorganization of the energy flows of the body.

When the Kundalini is fully awakened, the force climbs up along the spinal cord (through the three channels *Idâ, Pingalâ,* and *Sushumnâ)* and bursts open as a firework fountain on the crown. Resulting in a pronounced expansion of consciousness and a blissful elation of the 'enlightened' person.

On its way to the crown, the Kundalini force has ramified to the other chakras and cleansed psychobiophysical blockades of organs and nerve centers.

Is it the result of the worldwide increasing success of relaxation- and other spiritual techniques? Anyway, transpersonal psychologists and researchers of mystic experiences have come to the conclusion that more and more individuals show spontaneous Kundalini symptoms.

But not only meditation can lead to Kundalini awakenings. In particular cases, an existential, emotional or physical crisis can also stimulate for an indefinite period of time the 'snake fire'. Kundalini awakenings have been connected with the near-death experience as well. If the spontaneous uprising of the Kundalini is problematic (that is, not complete), the surprised yogi can be confronted with annoying physical and psychical side effects.

Often, the (mostly temporary) symptoms cannot be discerned from a genuine psychosis. Researchers of mystical experiences have repeatedly warned psychiatrists for misdiagnosis: it is a fact that many cases of Kundalini awakening have been sent to the lunatic asylum by uninformed doctors!

**Anomalies**
A wide range of psychobiophysical irregularities can be indicative of Kundalini activity. From subtle to fairly spectacular; there are different gradations in the symptoms. Most often, they are limited to one power boost and the positive and negative effects will disappear rapidly. A complete Kundalini process, with a permanent expansion of consciousness, is very rare.

If the symptoms appear without previous notice, they can elicit intolerable fear.

The victim frequently experiences an unusual pain in the back and the head. He does not feel well and can suffer from emotional outbursts. His limbs make involuntary movements or spontaneously take on yoga stances *(asanas)*.

Like the Human Batteries, many cases of Kundalini report disturbing interactions with electric devices. Vibrations, tingling and abnormal sensations of warmth spread over the whole body. Occasionally, an alarming, objectively measurable heat is observed.

The groundbreaking American researcher Lee Sannella, who died in 2010, described the Kundalini experience as a 'spiritual opening'. The occasional abnormal heat reminded him of anecdotes of Islamic Sufis. The state of 'enlightenment' that they experience is called by the Sufis 'the Fire of Separation'. It concerns a sort of depersonalization or complete detachment, during which intense body warmth is produced. Touching such a Sufi may cause serious burn injuries, and water poured on his hands would immediately evaporate!

Psychiatrist (and eye surgeon) Sannella also told the story of a 44-year-old bookseller who, one day, was meditating with her hands on the table. Suddenly she lost consciousness. When she came back to her senses, she noticed that her hands had left a burned imprint on the table-leaf! The same woman also developed every couple of months a sort of oval-form stigma on her forehead.

Of course, these stories fall under the category 'I'll believe it when I see it'…

The most decisive psychobiophysical characteristic of Kundalini activity is the 'subjective' observation of a luminous halo around one's genitals and spinal cord. When the power explosion is stronger, even a genuine pulsating light ball is seen around the head. Witnesses would have observed such light auras objectively; undoubtedly the traditional golden nimbus around the head of Christian and Oriental saints.

Other effects are spiritual gifts or *siddhis,* the hearing of voices (but not as threatening as for schizophrenics) and typical noises, such as the sound of thunder and the tinkling of bells. Furthermore, development of telepathic abilities and clairvoyance in time and space, the speaking and writing in foreign languages, healing by laying on of hands, and also significantly increased compassion and serenity.

**Prana**
The French NDE-expert Jean-Pierre Jourdan pointed, in a paper published in the *Journal of Near-Death Studies* (1994), to the similarity between the Kundalini symptoms and the psychobiophysical effects that accompany other numinous experiences: NDE, yoga- and Tao transcendence, shamanism and Hesychasm (more about the latter in the next chapter).

The shaman of the Iglulik Eskimos, for instance, is familiar with the manifestation of *quameneq:* a fire or a light that all of a sudden penetrates through the body and mind and that is said to, literally and figuratively, clear up the darkness. Paranormal side effects experienced by the shaman are clairvoyance in space and time, body separation, and the seeing of invisible creatures (who, themselves, will notice the shaman during his quameneq experience!).

Doctor Jourdan stated that control of the breathing plays a central role in the techniques used worldwide to stop the thinking and expand the consciousness.

The acceleration or slowing down of breathing elicits theta-waves in the neocortex-hippocampus circuit. This has a specific – and in the long run persistent – influence on the neuronal network and the nervous system. When Kundalini is activated unforeseenly, this characteristic breathing pattern would appear spontaneously.

In the Old Indian tradition, the *prana* or vital energy is synonymous with breath. A link that also was made with the *ruah* in the Old Testament and the *pneuma* in the New Testament (John 20:22):
'... *When he had said this, he breathed on them and said to them, "Receive the Holy Spirit".*'

There exists a breathing technique called *pranayama*, a rather risky method to awaken the snake fire (a link with the asthmatic light devotees of the previous chapter?).

The term prana, we are told, refers to the all-pervading cosmic energy, but also to the subtle bio-energy that streams through the whole body (corresponding to the Chinese *chi* or *qi*, the Japanese *ki* and the Tibetan *lung*).

By extreme concentration, the experienced yogi can draw prana from his most important organs and lead the force to his brain. Resulting in an expanded consciousness.

**Scientific research**
The Old Indian Tantric model describes the Kundalini process as a forced deviation of sexual energies from the genital area along the spinal column to the brain. This leads to a spiritual rebirth.

The increased number of people who demonstrate these ancient Kundalini symptoms, has encouraged the clinical observations in scientific circles. American researchers such as Itzhak Bentov and Lee Sannella acquired a certain reputation in this domain. As Dr Jourdan, also these scientists noticed the common 'illumination characteristics' described in so many different cultures. They showed that there is a fundamental, albeit sometimes difficult to discern, difference between the Kundalini effects and psychiatric illnesses, such as psychosis (a difference that lies especially in the overwhelming turmoil of the psychotic).

After serious laboratory work, Bentov, inventor and biomedical engineer, who died in 1979, developed a scientific theory that he called the physio-Kundalini model. Bentov argued that the neurobiological mechanism of Kundalini does not need supernatural interventions, yet can indeed have a consciousness expanding effect. The physical and emotional sensations of the person concerned can be coupled objectively with correlating brain activities.

Itzhak Bentov, who practised meditation himself, asserted that daily meditation can provoke the activation and stimulation of five synchronized bio-oscillators (producing high-frequency vibrations). Rhythmic pressure waves, originating from the interaction between the rhythm of the heart, the respiration, and subtle brain movement, can induce pulsating magnetic fields and circular flows around the two brain hemispheres. During this process, specific brain lobes are successively stimulated, which on their turn activate corresponding reactions in the body.

The Japanese scientist Hiroshi Motoyama (deceased in 2015) was a specialist in oriental medicine, a practised yogi, and even a Shinto priest! Motoyama experienced the Kundalini process himself. He wanted to examine methodically the subtle energies generated during this process, and developed for this purpose new electronic measuring instruments.

Motoyama maintained that a well-defined tension field can be measured around awakened or activated chakras. With his photon counter he could register, at these specific sites, the outburst of a high concentration of photons *i.e.* light particles, indicating a strong energy creation (cf. the findings of Doctor Beverly Rubik regarding the human biofield).

Moreover, Motoyama was convinced that the ancient and well-known *chi* or *ki* is actually the Grand Unified Force, that the physicists are still looking for today (force already predicted by the physicist Faraday in 1860 and identified as the Kabbalistic Astral Light by the occultist H.P. Blavatsky). For Motoyama, the subtle *prana* would lie at the basis of the weak, the strong, the electromagnetic and the gravity force.

Could herein lie the explanation of the frequently reported levitations of enlightened saints and yogis? And for Jesus' excursions on the water and his later ascension?

To finish, a caution from Frits Staal in his book *Exploring Mysticism: A Methodological Essay* (1975):
*'Despite the impressive amount of detailed research that has been performed in the study of yoga and of mysticism in general, and which used EEGs, ECGs and other similar methods, one has the impression that these studies approach their subject in much the same way as if one*

*would analyze paintings by filming the eye movements of the people who look at these paintings. Even if the results are correct, they are of minimal relevance.'*

## Gopi Krishna

One of the most renowned persons in recent history to have passed the entire Kundalini process is the Indian Gopi Krishna (1903-1984). In his autobiography *Kundalini: The Evolutionary Energy in Man* (1967) Krishna has described the progression of his Kundalini 'awakening' since its first manifestation in December 1937. From the meticulous analysis of his own case, we come to know Krishna as an exceptionally intelligent, informed, and integer man. What he tells us deserves the attention of everybody interested in the fundamental questions of life.

Krishna's superb adventure offers us nothing less than a concrete escape from the physicalist world view, that has gradually become inflexible.

*'(…) Kundalini,'* he writes, *'is the real cause of all genuine spiritual and psychic phenomena (…) the secret origin of all esoteric and occult doctrines (…) the fountainhead of all religious faiths, past, present and future.'*

Gopi Krishna spent his early years in Lahore (in the Punjab of British India), where he studied in a British college. He later returned to Jammu in northern India and worked as a civil servant for the government. At the age of thirty-four, his monotonous life was radically changed one morning, while he was beginning his regular meditation practice in front of his bedroom window.

After a few minutes of deep concentration on an imaginary lotus flower above the crown of his head, he experienced an unusual, but pleasant sensation at the base of his spine. The feeling came and went a couple of times, seemed to rise along his cervical column, and suddenly:

*'(…) with a roar like that of a waterfall, I felt a stream of liquid light entering my brain through the spinal cord (…) The illumination grew brighter and brighter, the roaring louder, I experienced a rocking sensation and then felt myself slipping out of my body, entirely enveloped in a halo of light (…) I felt the point of consciousness that was myself growing wider, surrounded by waves of light (…) I was no longer myself, or to be more accurate, no longer as I knew myself to be, a small point of awareness confined in a body, but instead was a vast circle of consciousness in which the body was but a point, bathed in light and in a state of exaltation and happiness impossible to describe.'*

After a while, things normalized and Krishna found himself back, sitting in lotus position in front of the bedroom window.

Soon afterwards, however, his physical condition began to deteriorate.

During the twelve years that followed this first overpowering Kundalini sensation, Krishna had to face alternating periods of utmost exaltation and pseudo-psychotic depression. The experience had such a profound effect on all the organs of his body that, at times, he walked as if he had been broken on a wheel.

His sufferings before reaching again his physical and psychical balance, were even enhanced by the lack of understanding in his social environment. The eccentricity and ineffability of this whimsical process made him feel, ever more, a Kafkian freak.

Gopi Krishna repeatedly emphasizes in his autobiography that he could not have survived the whole experience without the help of his wife. Throughout the years, she showed understanding and patience for his labile and disturbing behaviour. His gratitude even became greater, as he noticed, in despair, that his self-evident affection for his family regularly melted as snow in the sun.

Gopi Krishna – who 'subjectively' kept feeling that his head was a pulsating light bulb – managed after fifteen years of meticulous self-observation (and with an appropriate diet) to cope with his extravagant experience and turn it into a positive one. Great was his surprise, when he gradually arrived at the conclusion that the odd and alarming agitations in his body were the natural and systematic survival reactions of a highly destabilized organism.

After an exhausting period of insomnia, his nightly dream world transformed into a space of Elysian beauty and beatitude. During the day he 'saw' behind the phenomenal reality (transformed into a psychedelic vision) the kaleidoscopic, protean-like whirling of a timeless and all penetrating Consciousness. The pulsating light cloud around his head synchronized with the indescribable expansion and contraction of his experiencing Self.

Although he had never been attracted to poetry before, he now effortlessly wrote inspired poems, even in languages he had never learned (a phenomenon meaningfully corresponding with the 'speaking in foreign languages' of the Apostles after the descent of the Holy Spirit at Pentecost!).

**Evolution**

In his awe-inspiring autobiography, Gopi Krishna analysed the amazing biological, social and metaphysical implications of his 'clarified' view on the world.

The uniqueness of his views lies in his translation of the doctrine, that was originally taught in the religion classroom, to the lessons in biology and chemistry. In his interpretation, biochemical principles have taken over from the merciful intervention of the *Shakti* or Creative force of Shiva.

For Gopi Krishna, the Kundalini awakening has to be understood as an elicited or spontaneous overproduction of inherently present biological forces in the human body. A rare mutation in the natural evolution process that was initiated by a 'Cosmic Intelligence'. Krishna considered his own case as a confirmation of the Old Indian conviction that an individual can run through the almost endless reincarnation cycle (the human evolution) in one life, when applying effective introspection techniques.

As all other animal species, man is continuously evolving. So far, he seems to have been – for good and for worse - the most successful species on a contemplative and creative level.

Gopi Krishna agrees with modern neurobiology that the human brain forms a psychobiophysical unit. But he thinks that this brain/consciousness is teleologically evolving towards a broader 'comprehension'. This increased spirituality will, surprisingly, be associated with a reduction of the familiar 'ego-feeling' and an increase in the ecstatic experience of unity.

The biological driving force (Kundalini or prana) for this development has been present, from the start, in the human body. In close relationship with the sexual drive, it has been active during the indefinitely long chain of human generations.

This concept is reminiscent of that of the thanatologist Hubert Larcher (who died in 2008), who directed the Institut Métaphysique International in Paris from 1977 to 1995. Dr Larcher speculated on the possible transmutation of the natural sunlight, via a long biological and psychical evolution, into a spiritual or divine Light. In the opinion of Larcher, this conversion was already taking place, from time to time, in spiritually developed individuals (luminous saints!).

Also for Gopi Krishna, the manifestation of a genius, saint, enlightened or mystic has everything to do with Kundalini, that reveals itself prematurely in these persons. In a distant future, all people will be geniuses. In our era, in which humanity risks destroying its own future by its reckless morality, Krishna even envisaged the possibility of accelerating this evolutionary process by a collective psychobiophysical intervention.

A remarkable parallel with these ideas is found in the writings of Kenneth Ring, Michael Grosso and other American and British academics who became famous for their NDE research. They think that such a psychospiritual evolution is already accelerating, proof the explosion of 'shamanistic initiations' such as the near-death experiences and the, in many aspects, resembling *Ufo-abductions*.

## Krishnamurti

The man who, more than anyone else, had insisted on a mutation of the human mind is Jiddu Krishnamurti (1895-1986). This sharp and deeply reflective Indian 'philosopher' is considered by many as the most integer and consequent spiritual leader of the 20$^{th}$ century. His words and behaviour are in many ways reminiscent of the equally radical and confronting Nazorean from Galilea.

Krishnamurti was born in 1895 in the south Indian village Madanapalle, as the eighth child of Brahmin parents. When he was thirteen, he was 'discovered' in Adyar, Madras, by C.W. Leadbeater, a controversial leader of the Theosophical Society. Leadbeater, who claimed clairvoyance, was impressed. Not so much by the physical appearance or the behaviour of the dreamy-eyed and weak boy (it is said that Krishnamurti at that time made a sick, almost mentally retarded impression), but more by the beauty of his *aura*, 'that contained no trace of selfishness'. Something to remember in the light of Krishnamurti's subsequent specific statements.

In the summer of 1922 begins for Krishnamurti, 26 years old, in a little house in Ojai (California), what will later be called 'the Process'. From August 3$^{rd}$ onwards, he starts meditating for 30 minutes a day on the Maitreya.

Two weeks later, he is forced to reduce this meditation to 15 minutes, because of increasing neck pain. His brother Nityananda, who is also present in Ojai, notices *'a painful lump of what seemed to be a contracted muscle, about the size of a large marble.'*

August 19th: the pain in the neck reaches a climax; Krishnamurti, albeit in a state of 'reduced awareness', keeps contact with his entourage. In the distance, on the road in front of the house, he watches a stonemason at work. Krishnamurti suddenly IS the mason; he IS his pickaxe, the stone blocks, the grass, the tree next to the man, the birds. He IS the dust, the noise, a passing carriage and the driver of the carriage:

*'(…) I was in everything, or rather everything was in me, inanimate and animate, the mountain, the worm, and all breathing things. All day long, I remained in this happy condition. I could not eat anything, and again at about six I began to lose my physical body, and naturally the physical elemental did what it liked; I was half unconscious.'*

August 20th: Krishnamurti does not tolerate anyone near him; he does not want to be touched by anybody:

*'(…) I could feel them in rather a curious way and their vibrations got on my nerves.'*

In the evening, he is very weak and exhausted, as if his head is filled with needles. The complex and often unbearable physical symptoms, such as an intense pain along his spine to his crown, are reminiscent of the Old Indian Kundalini effects.

In 1930, Jiddu Krishnamurti explicitly took his distance from the Theosophical Society. The Truth, so he said, is a 'country without paths', that can only be found by personally searching for it.

From then on, Krishnamurti travelled ceaselessly around the world to bring his personal message. This message did not change in the course of the years and consists of the following guidelines: do not lean on a recognized authority in your quest for the Truth, let go the past and free your mind from psychological thinking. Because all disharmony, emotional suffering, and inability to make peace and true love are based on useless and inefficient thoughts. In the opinion of Krishnamurti, this spiritual transformation cannot be acquired gradually, but needs a change that has to take place here and now. Or never.

*'I know the way out of this everlasting misery,'* Krishnamurti said, *'and I want to help the people to get out of this pool of sorrow.'*

## The Infinite

At the end of his life, realizing that despite his years of touring, nobody seemed to really understand him, Krishnamurti began to fear he was a sort of unique mutation, especially with respect to the emptiness of his brain, the 'observing' without thinking and the capturing of the 'force'. Since his early childhood, he asserts, his mind had been void, without thoughts. Except when he was in conversation with persons around him, or when he was writing. He repeatedly expressed his astonishment about this emptiness.

*'(…) This was already the case when he was still a boy,'* he noted about himself, *'he didn't think. He just looked and listened, and that was it.'*

As a child at school, Krishnamurti was beaten almost daily. He was often sent out of the classroom: his inability to study, to remember something, was dismissed by his teachers as extreme laziness.

When referring to the 'force' that was present during the Process and later, Krishnamurti spoke in terms of 'the infinite', 'the sacred', 'the unknowable immensity', 'the other'. When *it* was there, he experienced it as ecstasy, bliss and joy.

And:

*'(…) The brain was completely empty; all reactions had stopped. During all these hours, I was unaware of the emptiness, that I only realized later while writing it down. But this knowledge is merely descriptive, it is not the essence.'*

As for his influence on others: what to think of the following testimony of one of Krishnamurti's acquaintances, the writer and yogi Vanda Scaravelli? Should we classify it as mere self-deception?

*'We were talking after lunch. No one was in the house. Suddenly K. (Krishnamurti) fainted. What happened then is impossible to describe, as there are no words that can come close to it; but it is also something that is too serious, too extraordinary, too important to be kept in the dark, buried in silence or not mentioned. There was a change in K.'s face. His eyes became larger and wider and deeper, and there was a tremendous look, beyond any possible state. It was as if there were a powerful presence which belonged to another dimension. There was an inexplicable feeling of emptiness and fullness at the same time.'*

Is this not reminiscent of Jesus the Nazorean's transfiguration on Mount Tabor? Besides, in spiritualist literature the term 'transfiguration' refers to the occasional transformation of the face of 'possessed' mediums in trance.

Krishnamurti declared, one day, having sometimes the impression of looking into the blazing desert sun with cut off eyelids…

And the 'powerful presence' sensed by Krishnamurti, is it perhaps identical to the Father, with whom Jesus said to be one?

Anyway, his words *'On that day you will know that I am in my Father, and you in me, and I in you'* (John 14:20) strongly suggest that the mystery of Jesus is related to his particular psychobiophysical constitution.

# VIII

# THE HESYCHASTS

In the previous chapters, I have looked for clues that can help us understand the mental and psychobiophysical particularities of Jesus. With this comparative material at hand, we now return to the actual subject of this book: the true origin of the Turin Shroud.

We have already asked ourselves the following question: how was it possible that the radiocarbon dating of 1988 pointed to an origin in the 13th or 14th century, whereas the sum of all the other research results of the Shroud had allowed for only one conclusion?

For most of the Catholic investigators, there is only one historical figure that could have fulfilled the spiritual and physiological conditions to make the inexplicable imprint on the Turin linen. Even the free-thinking skeptic has to admit that the imprint represents, in an unexplained way, this person. Our Western timetable starts with the birth of this man; both the canonical and the apocryphal Gospels bear witness of his supernormal talents.

To quote the words of STURP member Dr Robert Bucklin, Los Angeles coroner:

*'The imprint on the Shroud is the one of Jesus (...) Taking into account all we know, to whom else could this have happened?'*

The always overlooked solution of the Shroud-riddle lies in this question: did a human faculty of this nature remain unique over the following centuries?...

When discussing certain particular numinous or sublime experiences with identical psychobiophysical effects, we have already briefly mentioned Hesychasm (Greek *Hesychia:* silence, quietude, serenity).

Hesychasm is a mystic praying technique that has been practised for more than fifteen centuries. Transmitted in the 4$^{th}$ century by the Christian Desert Fathers in Egypt, by monks on Mount Sinai, and later by Eastern Orthodox anchorites.

The Eastern Orthodox Church originated around the turn of the first millennium, when the Byzantine Church separated from the Roman Catholic (1054: The Great East-West Schism). Main causes: increasing politicizing of the papal function and a seven centuries old dispute on the Divine Trinity.

Since that time, Hesychasm has been practised exclusively by the very conservative Mount Athos monks. Nowadays, about 1500 monks still live on the famous peninsular Holy Mountain in North-Eastern Greece (only a few are actual Hesychasts). They are spread over twenty-five fortified monasteries, situated in idyllic surroundings. After a relatively long period of decline, currently there is a surprising revival of these communities.

Children, women and female animals are not allowed in this semi-autonomous monastic republic (endowed with a special administrative status): for the monks,

Mount Athos is the exclusive Garden of the *Theotokos*, the Mother of God. The peninsula of Athos can only be reached by boat, solely by men and under strict access conditions.

Each year, on August 6th of the Julian calendar, the Athonites have their *Metamorphosis* celebration. The mystical, glorified Christ of the Transfiguration has always remained a central theme in the Byzantine Orthodox Church, in contrast to the crucified Saviour for the Roman Catholics.

During a night-time wake on the top of the 2033 m high mountain, the monks and pilgrims commemorate with prayer and ritual chanting the prefiguration of Christ's Resurrection: the Transfiguration of Jesus on Mount Tabor.

According to a local tradition, Athos is the actual Mount of Temptation. Another legend relates how Jesus' mother Mary, sailing to Cyprus, landed accidentally on the peninsula after a storm.

The doctrine of Hesychasm, central in the Orthodox Athos mystique, teaches that a detached lifestyle and a particular meditation technique can, by perseverance, induce a concrete mystical Light inside and outside the physical body of the experienced practitioner. This blissful Light is identified by the Hesychasts as the Transfiguration Light radiated by Jesus. And by extension, the Uncreated Divine Light (the *Shekinah* in the rabbinic theology).

As stated by Hesychasm, the gifted monk does not experience at that moment the essence *(ousia)* or the eternal, immaterial and unknowable being of the Almighty, but, in the first place, His active energy *(energeia)* or force.

Yet this energy can be identified with God himself, as it concerns his Uncreated and hence endless Light, as opposed to the created natural light.

This is why the Hesychast speaks of a *theosis*, which refers both to his feeling of Unison with God and to the deification of his physical body. Indeed, as stated by Athanasius of Alexandria:

'*God became man, for man to become God.*'

What actually is experienced, is the Evangelical holy spirit, the *pneuma agion*, that descended on the Apostles as fiery tongues, ten days after Christ's ascension.

The incomprehensible, boundless, eternal, and formless Light is, in the first place, perceived with the inner eye of the Hesychast. But occasionally also with the physical eyes of a receptive or casual witness…

## Breathing technique

The method used by the Hesychasts to generate the Light is similar to the Sufi- and yoga techniques aiming to neutralize and transcend the conditioned ego: quieting the mind, controlling the breathing process, concentration and contemplation.

Silencing the thoughts is promoted by continuously repeating the so called Prayer to Jesus or the Prayer of the Heart:

'Lord Jesus Christ, Son of God, have mercy on me.' *(Kyrie, Christe, eleison)*

Especially in its Latin form, this repetitive prayer may have the same elating effect as the Hindu mantra, though an Orthodox monk would not be pleased to hear this. The parallel with the *dhikr*-breathing technique of the Sufi cannot be a mere coincidence either;

to stay willfully aware of Allah, his name or a short religious text is repeated endlessly.

Both the mystically oriented Sufi and the Greek-Orthodox Hesychast aim to liberate the *noûs* (mind, cognizance, the spiritual organ for Divine perception) from the deluding thinking, imagination, reasoning, and fantasizing.

For the Hesychasts the noûs was initially localized in the heart, but after the Fall of Adam it spread over the whole body. Bringing back the noûs to the heart creates an intuitive openness *(metanoia)*. This openness brings a spiritual breakthrough and enables the beholding *(epopteia)* of the Divine Light.

Hesychasm is a technique that has an effect similar to the one obtained in the antique Mysteries and in the near-death experience. Blavatsky's comment on the Mysteries (see Chapter III) seems to confirm this:

'(...) *In essence, it* (the initiation) *represents this stage of divine clairvoyance, in which all that belongs to the earth disappears, the earthly face is paralyzed and the soul, free and pure, is united with his Spirit or God* (...) *The Spiritual Ego can only perform its action, when the personal ego is paralyzed.*'

Moreover, the blessed Hesychast (only one in ten thousand is said to reach his goal) receives the famous Pauline gifts, similar to the *siddhis* of the yogi or the *karama* of the Sufi: telepathy, clairvoyance and so on.

For the Hesychast, Sufi, mystes and yogi the assistance of an experienced spiritual guide is crucial. The path towards transrational knowledge is not without danger: spiritual mistakes can lead to ego-inflation, madness and suicide.

## Symeon the New Theologian

The Hesychasts rely for their mystical activities on some of the early Church Fathers and on the spirituality of unconventional desert hermits (Clement of Alexandria, Macarius of Syria, Dionysius Areopagites and others).

*'Like the inner Glory of Christ,'* the 4$^{th}$ century author of the *Macarius Homilies* writes, *'(on Mount Tabor) covered his body and cleared it completely, so will the force of Christ in the heart of the saints stream over their body'...*

A holy man of such calibre was apparently Symeon who became known as the New Theologian, the actual initiator and theoretician of the Greek Hesychast movement.

Symeon was born in 949 CE in Paphlagonia (an area on the Black Sea coast of north-central Anatolia) into the Byzantine nobility. As a young man, he went to Constantinople aiming to make a political career. Initially, he served important patricians and led a rather careless life.

His religious nature brought him to the then famous monastery of Stoudios, where he met Symeon the Studite (from whom he took on his name; his name at birth remains unknown). The extraordinary experiences with the Studite led him to believe that a personal contact with the living God was still possible, and not a closed case of the Old and New Testament times.

*'Do not say,'* Symeon the New Theologian later wrote, *'that it is impossible to receive the Spirit of God... Do not say that God does not manifest Himself to man. Do not say that men cannot perceive the divine light, or that it is impossible in this age! Never is it found to be impos-*

*sible, my friends. On the contrary, it is entirely possible when one desires it.'* (Hymn 27, 125-132)

In his *Discourses* he remembers:

'*(...) You already live in him* (that is, in his mentor Symeon the Studite) *and shine in him with Divine Glory. So I kneeled before him and looked up at him with faith and repentance. Suddenly, I perceived a Divine warmth. Then a small radiance that shone forth. Then a Divine breath from his words. Then a fire kindled in my heart, which caused constant tears to flow. After that, a fine beam went through my mind more quickly than lightning. Then appeared to me as it were a light in the night, and a small flaming cloud rested on his head, while I hid my face and prayed. Then it disappeared, and soon thereafter it seemed to be in heaven.*'

Symeon the Studite became the personal teacher of Symeon the New Theologian on his mystical path.

Speaking of himself in the third person, Symeon the New Theologian describes his first personal experience with the Light:

'*(...) During the day, he managed a patrician's household and daily went to the palace, engaged in worldly affairs, so that no one was aware of his pursuits. One day, as he stood and recited "God, have mercy upon me, a sinner...", uttering it with his mind rather than his mouth, suddenly a flood of divine radiance appeared from above and filled all the room. As this happened, the young man lost all awareness (of his surroundings) and forgot that he was in a house or that he was under a roof. He saw nothing but light all around him and did not know if he was standing on the ground. He was not afraid of falling: he was not concerned with the world nor did anything pertaining to men and corporeal beings enter his mind. Instead, he seemed to himself to have turned into light. Oblivious of the entire world, he was filled with tears and with ineffable joy and gladness. His mind then ascended to heaven and beheld yet another light, which was clearer than that which was close at hand.'*

(Compare this with the assertion of the shaman Aua, Iglulik Eskimo, around 1900:

*'And during this fit of mysterious and overwhelming ecstasy I became a shaman (…) I could see and hear in a totally different way. I had acquired my quameneq, my enlightenment, the shaman light of body and brain.'*)

Very rapidly, Symeon the New Theologian understood that he owed this grace to his teacher:

*'(…) Through our teacher Symeon* (the Studite), *God has also glorified us, his brothers. Symeon gave us the Holy Spirit.'*

The young monk had 'drunk and washed himself in the living water of Christ, streaming from Symeon the Studite'.

In 976, Symeon the New Theologian entered as a novice in the monastery of Stoudios. Already four years later, he was nominated abbot of the Mammas monastery in the Byzantine capital. The rule he imposed on his monks – nowadays followed less strictly by modern Athonites – was fairly Spartan. In 1009, he retired as a simple monk in Chrysopolis (on the Asian shore of Constantinople), where he died thirteen years later, aged 73.

**Etheric light**

The 'psychosomatic technique' that Symeon taught his monks, was summarized by himself in these words (the text has recently also been attributed to Nicephorus the Hermit):

> '(…) *Then sit down in a quiet cell, in a corner by yourself, and do what I tell you. Close the door, and withdraw your intellect from everything worthless and transient. Rest your beard on your chest, and focus your physical gaze, together with the whole of your intellect, upon the center of your belly or your navel. Restrain the drawing-in of breath through your nostrils, so as not to breathe easily, and search inside yourself with your intellect so as to find the place of the heart, where all the powers of the soul reside. To start with, you will find there darkness and an impenetrable density. Later, when you persist and practise this task day and night, you will find, as though miraculously, an unceasing joy. For as soon as the intellect attains the place of the heart, at once it sees things of which it previously knew nothing. It sees the open space within the heart and it beholds itself entirely luminous and full of discrimination.*'

> '*God is fire*,' Symeon clarifies in another text, '*and He is called this by all inspired scripture, while the soul of each of us is a lamp. Now a lamp, before it receives a flame and is lit, is completely in darkness, even if it's full of oil, tow or other combustible matter (…) Those whose lamp of the soul is still like this – that is, untouched by the divine fire – are in greater need of a guide with a torch, somebody who'll discern their actions.*'

As Macarius of Syria in the 4th century had already done before him, Symeon warned for possible misunderstanding of this type of metaphor:

*'When you hear the words 'light of knowledge' do not think it is only about the knowledge of what is being said and not about the actual light… There is no other way to reach the knowledge of God than by seeing the light that he is sending.'*

For the uninitiated, it is hard to grasp the meaning of all this. Whereas the Greco-Roman mystes, who had been confronted with a near-death experience, would easily have understood the following assertion of Symeon:

*'A man who is ONE with God, sees things that I am not allowed to disclose. His spirit perceives strange visions and is illuminated and becomes the light itself. And this light lives and gives light to those who see it. He finds himself completely united with the light. And he concentrates on the vision, and he is what he was. He discerns the light in his soul and becomes entranced. And in this trance, he sees the light from far away, but when he comes back to himself, he finds himself in the middle of the light. He has no words or understanding to describe what he has seen in his vision.'*

Symeon emphasizes the physical part of the sensation. He affirms that even profane mortals can witness this numinous Light:

*'The bodies of saints can take part in the divine fire, and they are glorified and glow. They become transparent, and are restored more exquisite and precious than other bodies.'*

In a testimony on the 'enlightened' Desert Father Abba Silvanus we read:

*'I saw his face and body radiate like an angel, and I fell down on the ground.'*

For Symeon, this was the final phase of a gradual immersion in the Divine Light of the now 'transfigured' monk.

*'The light shines in me like a radiant lamp,'* declares the jubilant Symeon.

It now becomes interesting to compare Symeon's words with Jesus' statement in Matthew 6:22-23:

*'The eye is the lamp of the body. So, if your eye is healthy* (or *single,* or *natural.* Greek: aploûs)*, your whole body will be full of light; but if your eye is unhealthy, your whole body will be full of darkness. If then the light in you is darkness, how great is the darkness!'*

In Luke 11:36, Jesus adds to this:

*'(…) If then your whole body is full of light, with no part of it in darkness, it will be as full of light as when a lamp gives you light with its rays.'*

What did the Nazorean mean by 'a healthy' or 'a single' or 'a natural' eye?

The story *De sera* of Plutarch (from his collection of essays *Moralia)* fits perfectly here.

This Greek contemporary of Paul tells us the story of Thespesios of Soles. Thespesios has a near-death experience after he had an unfortunate fall on his head. Abruptly, he leaves his body and briefly ends up in a multicoloured world, whirling with energy. He now can move in all directions with an incredible ease and speed. Moreover, Thespesios can observe this whole world of light 'as with one eye'…

The *kalyves* are small, derelict monasteries occupied by about five monks, located in a hardly accessible area on Athos, called 'the desert'. In this region still live a few solitary anchorites who practise Hesychasm in its extreme form. On their guard for indiscreet eyes and living of gifts of food and rainwater.

A few curious rucksack tourists have managed to stand eye to eye with them. Some have affirmed they felt, at that moment, a sort of electrical discharge flowing through their body…

**Gregory Palamas**
The Orthodox Light Mystique had its peak in the 14$^{th}$ century. The man who voiced successfully the Hesychast doctrine in the entire Byzantine Empire was an Athos monk, Gregory Palamas (1296-1359), later Bishop of Thessaloniki.

From 1338 onwards, Palamas defended in Constantinople the Hesychast movement against the attacks of Barlaam. This southern Italian monk and scholar from Calabria, was abbot of the Basilian monastery of the Byzantine capital, under the reign of Emperor Andronicus III (1328-1341).

The Roman Catholics and their Byzantine brothers in faith had mutually excommunicated each other in 1054. In contrast to Palamas, Barlaam advocated a return to the Latin Church. But above all, Barlaam was a fanatic anti-Hesychast. He considered their mystical methods an absurd superstition and accused Palamas of heresy. Had the Athos monk not claimed to have seen the eternal God with his own eyes?

Barlaam dismissed the Hesychast claims on theological grounds. He had been influenced by the Neo-Platonists, and he was a typical adept of the rational, scholastic theology. Hence his conclusion that God was completely transcendental, and of an absolutely inaccessible nature. This excluded any form of divine contemplation or unity experience.

Moreover, the Hesychasts asserted that this Union with God could be experienced physically here and now! For Barlaam, an admirer of Plato, the human physicality was inferior, whereas the Hesychasts had returned to the Old-Jewish notion of a unity between the soul and the physical body.

Gregory Palamas admitted that the essence of the Eternal was unthinkable and could not be attained; but that this was not the case for His uncreated energy or active force (perceptible as Light). By leading an ascetic and contemplative life, the prepared mystic could be overwhelmed by this Uncreated Light and become 'transfigured'.

Here, the theological doctrine and the clever speculations about God had been replaced by the totally new perspective of *metanoia*, the inner experience of His Endless Presence.

## Patriarchal councils

On June 10$^{th}$ 1341, patriarch John XIV Kalekas held a council in Constantinople on the Hesychast issue. The public discussions between Palamas and Barlaam took place in the Haghia Sophia Cathedral and were presided by the Byzantine Emperor Andronicus III. The heated debate was won by the Hesychasts.

Shortly thereafter a civil war broke out. When the Roman Catholic oriented patriarch Kalekas became regent – Andronicus III had died and the new Emperor John V was only 8 years old at that time – he had Gregory Palamas, who had stayed neutral in the conflict, incarcerated for four years.

The Hesychast debate deteriorated soon into a bitter fight between political rivals: proponents and opponents of the ruling emperors. There was even for a short time a Hesychast party! Palamas resisted the philosophical, theological and political attacks of the Barlamites. The Hesychasts remained influential during the next five synods, partly because of their obstinate anti-Catholic stance. Despite the initial opposition of some patriarchs, over time the resistance dwindled, and ultimately Palamist doctrine became accepted throughout the Eastern Orthodox Church.

The whole dispute entered the history books as the *Hesychast Controversy.*

Gregory Palamas died in 1359; his last words were: *Heaven, Heaven, Up to Heaven!* Later he was sanctified as Father and Doctor of the Eastern Orthodox Church. As with many visionaries who had been in contact with mystical light phenomena during their lifetime, his body was found almost intact when exhumed many years later...

Up to the present day, the Hesychast Transfiguration doctrine is a dogma for the Eastern Orthodox Church. Barlaam left for Calabria, where he converted to the Roman Catholic Church and was appointed Bishop of Gerace.

Interestingly, the *Catholic Encyclopedia* refers online to the Hesychast claims as 'obscure speculations' and 'extravagant mysticism'.

**Kingdom of God**
According to the Roman Catholic Faith, Jesus' famous Kingdom of God – a term the Nazorean probably adopted from John the Baptist – refers to Christ's glorious Second Coming and his Kingdom at the end of times.

Gregory Palamas, however, asserted that a correct understanding of the intriguing Transfiguration story in Mark 9, leads to the conclusion that God's Kingdom is identical with the Light radiating from Jesus' body on Mount Tabor. Hence, identical with the Uncreated Divine Light.

This Uncreated Light is different from the natural light, that can be observed by the senses. The question then arose how the chosen Apostles Peter, John and James on Mount Tabor suddenly could see the Light – in the opinion of Palamas present from the start in Jesus, but generally invisible to the physical eye. Because, Palamas said, their eyes were sanctified at that moment by the Spirit.

As Jesus had promised six days earlier, the three disciples received the Grace of the Light:
*'Among those who stand here, some* (i.e. Peter, John and James) *will not die before they have seen in all its power the Kingdom of God.'*

Probably meaning that the disciples received Jesus' 'baptism with the Holy Spirit'. Like Symeon the New Theologian, when he stood close to his 'enlightened' teacher Symeon the Studite.

On very rare occasions, however, even a surprised (and certainly astounded) bystander can witness the Hesychast Transfiguration Light.

Because, Gregory Palamas writes,

*'Even the physical body participates in one way or the other in the glory that has been activated in the noûs. And the body even feels something of the inexpressible mystery that is flowing from here to the soul.'*

This reminds us inevitably of the amazing testimonies of the radiant and glowing saints discussed in Chapter VI.

If we may believe the Orthodox Archbishop Hierotheos Vlachos, even today a few Hesychast monks on Mount Athos sleep with a radiating face. Is there a connection with the Italian devotee Anna Monaro, whose chest emitted light while she was asleep?

*'He who can make glow the firefly,'* Saint Cyril of Jerusalem said, *'can bring light to the just even more.'*

### Reanimating force

Before we pass to the true origin of the Turin Shroud, let us go back, for a moment, to the 1st century.

Much indicates that the charismatic Nazorean had discovered within himself a specific (life- and light giving) power source from which he could tap at will. Jesus called this metaphysical or numinous source God's Kingdom. On Mount Tabor he gave three of his Apostles a 'foretaste' of it.

This preternatural force enabled him to successfully heal certain physical and mental illnesses of his fellow men. Even to reanimate some who were clinically dead.

Is it possible that he trusted his (apparently very effective) power so much that he wanted to use it for himself in due time? Perhaps Jesus' predictions about his own death and resurrection have to be understood in the light of his multifaceted 'power' and his unwavering belief in it.

*'As they were coming down the mountain, he ordered them to tell no one about what they had seen, until after the Son of Man had risen from the dead. So they kept the matter to themselves, questioning what this rising from the dead could mean.'* (Mark 9:9-10)

Was the later resurrection belief of his stunned Apostles only a consequence of the bold claims that Jesus had made? Of his smart, persuasive art and questionable hocus-pocus?

Or did Jesus with his own 'energetic force' – under some conditions he had discussed before with a few of his confidants – actually reanimate for an undetermined period of time his own clinically dead and not too mutilated body?...

*'I praise you, Father, Lord of heaven and earth,'* spoke the Nazorean, *'because you have hidden these things to the wise and intelligent and have revealed them to the little children.'*

Perhaps the already mentioned testimony of eleven-year-old Joe, rather than the prejudiced speculations of any believer or skeptic, can help us to discover the true facts that happened during Jesus' transfiguration and resurrection.

According to pediatrician Melvin Morse, the clinically dead boy saw his body lying on the bed, surrounded by a soft white light.

*'I heard a sizzling sound,'* the reanimated kid later told, *'and before I knew, I was squatting against a corner of the ceiling. I saw my body down below, emitting light as if I had a light bulb in me...'*

Let us compare Joe's story with the testimony of Giuseppe Costa, reported by his friend, the Italian parapsychologist Ernesto Bozzano (1862-1943).

One night, engineer Costa almost suffocated in his bedroom because of a problem with a paraffin lamp:

*'(...) I had the clear and precise sensation of finding myself with only my thinking personality, in the middle of the room, completely separated from my body, which continued to lie in bed. I saw – if I may call this sensation that way – the objects around me as if a visible radiation of molecules penetrated the objects to which I turned my attention, as if matter dissolved with my thinking. I saw my body perfectly recognizable in all its details, the profile, the figure, but with the clusters of veins and nerves vibrating like a swarm of luminous living atoms (...) Then I thought of my mother, who was sleeping in the next room. I saw her clearly through the dividing partition, quietly asleep in her bed. But her body seemed to irradiate, in a different way from my body, something shining, a phosphorescent glow...'*

# IX

# THE ATHOS SHROUD

First, a short note on the history of Athos.

Athos, one of the three headlands to the South of the Greek peninsula Chalcidice, had become more and more deserted since the beginning of the Christian era. Around 800 CE, the wild, wooded promontory became again inhabited, this time by anchorites or Christian hermits. These pious men lived a reclusive and ascetic life, alone or in small communities. Fasting and praying were their main activities.

In 833, Athos received the special protection of Basil I. The Byzantine Emperor wanted the Athonites to have absolute peace for dedicating themselves to mysticism; he forbade all bureaucratic intervention on the small peninsula. At that moment, the empire had been in turmoil for about one hundred years by the dispute whether holy *images* could or could not be venerated (the *iconoclasm*).

In 908, the Emperor nominated a Primate for Athos. Until 1312, the Primate was a sort of governor and representative.

In 942, Emperor Romanos I Lecapenos offered a genuine yearly salary (of one gold coin) to every Athonite.

Around that time, Symeon the New Theologian (see Chapter VIII) was born near Sinope.

Twenty years later the construction of the Big Lavra, the first organized monastery of Athos, was started at the foot of the Mountain. Athanasius of Trebizond received the needed finances and privileges from his friend Emperor Nicephorus Phocas. The Lavra became a prosperous religious community, with its own farmland and vineyards. Not surprisingly, this created resistance among the ragged and solitary anchorites.

Shortly thereafter, Emperor John Tsimiskis offered a Charter to the Athonites. It was a juridical document with economical rules and guidelines, destined to guarantee the peaceful coexistence of the monks and the hermits.

In 978, the Georgian noble Ioannis Tornikios founded the Iveron monastery. He received for this the grateful support of Emperor Basil II, whom had been freed by Tornikios from his rival Barlas Scleros.

Again, the local hermits were very displeased. After the construction of the spacious and attractively situated Vatopediou Monastery in 1020, the organized monastic life came into full bloom. In 1045, Athos received its official name of *Agio Oros* or Holy Mountain.

Nine years later, in 1054, the Great Schism separated Constantinople from Rome.

Constantine IX Monomachos imposed new rules for Athos, especially concerning the economic activities of the monasteries. Their success became very influential in whole Byzantium, particularly because of the favourable geographical localization of the peninsula. The monasteries had their own ship and could sail the

Mediterranean See, that was again fairly safe after the reconquest of Crete on the Arabs.

Later, monasteries were created by people that were not Greek Byzantine (Russians, Bulgari, and Serbians). The doctrines concerning religious matters that developed within the monastic walls, became more and more significant for the Orthodox world.

Meanwhile, the Byzantines, threatened by the Latin Crusaders, tried to defend their Empire. After the Fourth Crusade against the Turks in 1204, Constantinople was taken by the Crusaders and their Venetian allies, and also Athos was occupied for a short time. Treasures were stolen, monasteries set on fire and monks persecuted. Inevitably, this increased the bitter hatred of Athos against the Church of Rome.

In 1274, the second Council of Lyon pleaded for a reunification of both religious parties. Emperor Michael VIII Palaeologus (who had reconquered Constantinople on the Crusaders in 1261) showed for obvious reasons his political interest. The conservative Athonites were outraged and rejected the proposal. Their hostility against the Roman 'modernism' grew day by day.

The peninsula had already suffered a lot from belligerent Mediterranean pirates. Moreover, in 1307, Spanish mercenaries of the Catalan (Crusader) Campaign in East Macedonia plundered the Orthodox monasteries. Nevertheless, on Athos the number of religious communities increased and the prestige of the Athonites kept growing.

Around that time began the Hesychast Controversy. The dispute on the Divine Transfiguration Light stirred up the entire Orthodox world…

**Vostitza**

In 1355, when the Hesychast crisis was at its peak, Jeanne de Vergy, widow of Geoffrey de Charny, displayed for the first time the Turin Shroud in the little French town of Lirey.

Ian Wilson and other dissident historians to this day remain convinced – in spite of the scientific carbon-14 dating – that the outlandish Turin Shroud is the authentic grave cloth of Jesus the Nazorean. Initially conserved doubled in four in Edessa in Asia-Minor (the Mandylion), the linen would have been kept from 942 to 1204 in the Church of St Mary of Blachernae in Constantinople.

The cloth would have disappeared without a trace after the disastrous Fourth Crusade, and circulated for 150 years in Byzantine Greece, before it surfaced in France.

After a military campaign in Greece, Wilson states, Geoffrey's older brother Dreux had married, in 1316, Agnes de Charpigny. She was the granddaughter of Crusader Hugh de Lille Charpigny and had inherited the barony of Vostitzia, in the northwest of the Peloponnese, then called the Latin Kingdom of Morea.

Ian Wilson – in accord with the French historian Joseph du Teil, who had proposed this hypothesis already in 1902 – has argued that the Shroud came into the possession of Geoffry de Charny via this Greek connection. Wilson speculates that the alleged Mandylion/Shroud of Jesus had been stolen by Hugh de Lille Charpigny from the Church of St. Mary of Blachernae in Constantinople and brought to his barony Vostitzia in Greece.

Interestingly, a letter of complaint written by Theodore Angelus Comnenus, member of the Byzantine imperial family, addressed to Pope Innocentius III on August 1st 1205, gives an alternative clue on the provenance of the Shroud.

Comnenus maintained that French crusaders appropriated in Constantinople *'the linen in which our Lord Jesus Christ was wrapped after his death and before the resurrection'* and sent it to Athens.

According to Prof. Daniel S. Scavone and other Shroud scholars, the Burgundian nobleman and crusader Othon de la Roche, Duke of Athens and Thebes since 1205, sent this cloth to his father Ponce de la Roche in Besancon. Ponce offered the relic to the Archbishop of this French town, where it was conserved in the local Church of Saint Etienne.

Jeanne de Vergy was the great-great-granddaughter of Othon de la Roche. The same scholars speculated that this was the nowadays Shroud, that would have ended up in Lirey after a fire in the Besancon Church.

Anyway, the connection between the unique present-day Shroud of Turin and the Charny family in Greece is very probable. But in my opinion, there is a more obvious explanation for the creation and the provenance of the controversial cloth than the hypotheses reviewed earlier in this book.

### Identical replication

Despite what skeptics may say, the Turin Shroud remains, up to the present day, a scientifically unexplained phenomenon. A *preternatural* relic: an artefact that, so far, cannot be explained for lack of information. Therefore, it is not unreasonable to hypothesize that the image was created by a yet unknown radiation, released by Jesus' 'resurrected' body. In Chapter I, I have cited the many Christian physicists who defend this hypothesis.

On the other hand, it is equally fair to accept that the Turin Shroud was in one way or another 'fabricated' in the 13$^{th}$ or 14$^{th}$ century. At least that is what the radiocarbon dating of 1988 determined.

Nonetheless, the particularly unusual nature of the controversial linen cannot be denied.

Indeed, all indicates that the *image* on the Shroud is an *identical replication,* not an artistic forgery. Meaning that the procedure by which it was made, could have been *the same* as the procedure that Jesus the Nazorean himself had applied much earlier, as described in the sermon of Pope Stephan III (8$^{th}$ century):

*'Indeed, it was the very mediator between God and man that laid himself down on a white sheet, to fulfil the wish of King Abgar* (the diseased King of Edessa). *The glorious image of the face and the whole body of the Lord were thus miraculously transferred onto it. So much, that those who could not see the Lord in person, could see his transfiguration on the fabric.'*

The Turin Shroud we know today surfaced in France in 1355.

Who claimed, in the period between 1338 and 1368 (as other Christian mystics had done much earlier), that they could awaken Jesus' Transfiguration Light within themselves?

Quite so! The Eastern Orthodox Hesychasts...

As already explained in the previous chapter, Hesychasm is a specific meditation technique by which the Universal Light can manifest itself in the body of a persevering practitioner. This ecstatic Light is identified by the Hesychasts as the Transfiguration Light of Jesus on Mount Tabor in Galilee.

1 Peter 3:18 asserts that the material of the fiery *pneuma agion* (holy spirit) is the same as that of Jesus' resurrection body. In Romans 8, Paul also explains that the spirit in Christ empowered his resurrection, and that all men can hope to live at the End of Times, provided they believe in God's or in Christ's spirit.

But the Hesychasts aimed the *visio dei luminis* (the vision of the divine light) and the (temporary) transfiguration of their body *before* their death, through the 'baptism with the Holy Spirit'. Symeon the New Theologian even said:

*'He who has not known God in this life, will not know Him in the following.'*

I have already drawn the attention to the exclusive character of this sublime experience: the ancient Mysteries also emphasized that the eternal life awaited only the initiated.

According to Paul, Jesus had publicly shown the *mystérion*. Yet Jesus has remained discreet: only to those who 'had ears to hear', the secrets of the Kingdom of God would be revealed.

This raises the question to what extent the current Roman Catholic Sacraments still represent truly the ancient Christian Mysteries. It looks as if the institutionalized churches have not understood Jesus' warning on 'the narrow gate and the hard road that leads to life' (Matthew 7:14).

*'God is light,'* Symeon wrote, *'An endless and unfathomable light, simple, not composed, timeless. The light is the immortality, the door to the Kingdom of Heavens. The light is the Kingdom itself (…)'*

A comparison of this Hesychastic experience with that of Jiddu Krishnamurti:

*'(…) It was light; thinking and feeling had no part of it, they could never give the light; they were not there, there was only light, as when the sun has sunken deep behind the city walls in a cloudless sky. You cannot see that light, unless you know the timeless movement of meditation, the end of thinking. Love is not the way of thinking and feeling (…)'*

Symeon the New Theologian had an intimate relation with this Sublime Light during all his adult life. He affirmed that he could see it, not only with 'his spiritual gaze of the mind', but also with his physical eyes.

*'Oh awesome miracle that I can see both ways, with my two pairs of eyes, those of the body and those of the soul.'*

## Seraphim of Sarov

The Hesychast literature mentions that occasionally even unprepared laymen can be the witness of a radiating Hesychast. The Eastern Orthodox world, for instance, loves to refer to the famous report of the 19th century business man and philosopher Nicolas Motovilov. This reluctant seeker registered his intimate conversation with the Russian forest recluse Seraphim of Sarov (1759-1833), a great *staretz*, seer and miracle worker of his time.

On a gloomy day in November 1831, during a discussion in the woods on how to acquire the Holy Spirit and the required state of mind, Motovilov once more expressed his doubts. Suddenly, Seraphim grasped him by the shoulders and forced him to look without fear into his eyes.

*'We ARE both in the completeness of the Spirit now,'* Seraphim said, *'Also you, otherwise you could not see me as I am now…'*

Motovilov continues his amazing account:

*'(…) After these words I glanced at his face, and there came over me an even greater reverent awe. Imagine in the center of the sun, in the dazzling light of its midday rays, the face of a man talking to you. You see the movement of his lips and the changing expression of his eyes, you hear his voice, you feel someone holding your shoulders. Yet you do not see his hands, you do not even see yourself or his figure, but only a blinding light spreading far around for several yards and illumining with its glaring sheen both the snow-blanket that covered the forest glade and the snowflakes that besprinkled the great Elder and me. You can imagine the state I was in!'*

Moreover, Motovilov became aware of a paradisiac scent. He had no words for the joy and unearthly peace that overtook him. In the end, he felt himself, despite the cold winter atmosphere, immersed in an intense and beneficent warmth, *'comparable to a steam bath on the moment the whirling vapours surround you'*.

Also Seraphim of Sarov described Jesus' Kingdom of God as 'standing in the wholeness of the Holy Spirit'. A state of mind, that the surprised and confused Motovilov was allowed to experience for one merciful moment.

Motovilov, apparently concerned that nobody would believe his report, ends with the following declaration:
*'The ineffable glow of the light which emanated from him* (Seraphim), *I myself saw with my own eyes. And I am ready to vouch for it with an oath.'*

In 1903, Tsar Nicolas II sanctified Seraphim in his birthplace. The ceremony was attended by none other than the notorious miracle worker Gregory Rasputin, who, besides, would have foretold on that occasion the birth of the future Tsarevich Alexei.

**Microwave radiation**

An 'enlightened' Hesychast remains extremely rare.

As rare as the image on the Turin Shroud?...

One thing is certain. The luminous *tour de force* that Jesus the Nazorean performed on Mount Tabor CAN apparently be repeated by an Orthodox Hesychast. Thus, the claim that the inexplicable photorealistic image on the Shroud can *only* have been produced by Jesus' unique physical resurrection, is flawed.

The radiocarbon dating, the year in which the Shroud (of Turin) appeared for the first time in France, and other significant data indeed point to the 13th and 14th century Greek Hesychasts.

But we must keep in mind that de Hesychast theology and (ritual) method became 'popular' (so to speak) from the days of Symeon the New Theologian, who lived in the tenth century. It is likely that cloths with a 'fiery imprint', other than the only and unique example we know today, already circulated in the Byzantine Empire for at least a few hundred years, as suggested by the following fragment of an inventory from 1201. Nicolas Mesarites, the keeper of the relics of the Pharos Chapel in the Boukoleon Palace in Constantinople, mentions:

> '(...) SHROUDS (sindones) *of Christ of cheap and ordinary linen. They still smell of myrrh and are indestructible since they covered the dead, naked and embalmed body after the Passion.*' [sic]

Is there, by the way, any reason to think that the conservative Orthodox monk of today differs in appearance from his medieval faith fellow? A modern tourist in Greece will notice to his surprise the likeness between the Orthodox monastery monk and the man on the Turin Shroud. Including the characteristic ponytail (only clearly visible on the original Shroud)!

The radiation model has proven, up to now, to be the most plausible model to explain the origin of the much-discussed imprint. So far the conclusion of Dr August D. Accetta and his colleagues, who experimented with nuclear medicine instruments. A volunteer was injected with the rapidly decaying isotope Technetium 99. The gamma rays captured from his naked body were artificially forced into parallel beams. The scanned nuclear image corresponded to a large extent with the image on the Turin Shroud.

If the radiation was of an electromagnetic nature, a microwave radiation with a wavelength between 0.3 and 1 mm seems to be the most plausible. For scientist

Bernard Power, a forceful and short dose of this type of radiation could have caused a super-hot evaporation of condensed water droplets on the humid fibres of the linen. Resulting in the characteristic local dehydration and yellowing of the fibre tips. However, the problem of the natural verticality of such radiation process remains unexplained for the time being.

Electromagnetic or not, the human body that once laid between the upper and lower part of the folded Turin Shroud, must somehow have emitted a strong radiation dose.

The Sublime Light? It has been seen repeatedly, even with the physical eyes of profane witnesses. This makes its visible interaction with the linen fabric even more plausible.

**Tachyonic field**
How does the Sublime Light relate to the natural light? As maintained by a thought-provoking scientific hypothesis, the *consciousness* forms the basis for both.

The French biophysicist Régis Dutheil and his daughter Brigitte Dutheil of the Medical Faculty of Poitiers developed the following fascinating theory. For them, the Superconsciousness (the Sublime Light or the Universal Information System) is a tachyonic phenomenon. Tachyons are hypothetical particles that can move faster than light.

For the Dutheils, the Superconsciousness can transform via a 'filter' in the brain cortex the images from an undifferentiated universe into a bio-individual, three-dimensional reality. When a person dies, the individual consciousness regains its properties of time and space (or more precisely the lack of them) which Einstein's special theory of relativity predicts for tachyonic speeds.

This reasoning seems to corroborate with the core elements of the famous near-death experience: annihilation of the linear time and causal relations, global spatial perception and unlimited and immediate processing of information.

The frequently reported rushing through the NDE tunnel would be the breaking of the light wall by the consciousness, which now has become Light itself. The panoramic flashback of one's individual history and the reliving of it, occasionally perceiving future events, etc.

For the Dutheils, the brain 'filter' exerts its restricting function throughout the whole life. During a far-reaching spiritual or mystical experience, there would be a more or less serious 'leakage' of that filter…

Basing himself on previous neurosurgical findings, the American pediatrician and NDE expert Melvin Morse has identified this 'filter' as the right temporal brain lobe. As already mentioned, Dr Morse calls this the *God Spot*. He is convinced that this spot can give direct access, be it natural or forced, to the Sublime Superconsciousness. With occasionally specific paranormal effects on the three-dimensional level…

With their theory, Régis and Brigitte Dutheil, and Melvin Morse have tried to explain rationally the perception of the mystical Light during a near-death experience. This concept is equally valid for the Light of the Mysteries, Kundalini, the shamans and the Hesychasts.

## Jospice Imprint

*'The Kingdom of God is among you,'* Jesus declared (Luke 17:21). The so called baptism with fire automatically followed after a specific state of consciousness was reached. This is what the reanimated adolescent in the Secret Gospel of Mark also experienced:

*'Jesus went off with her into the garden where the tomb was, and straightway, going in where the youth was, he stretched forth his hand and raised him, seizing his hand. But the youth, looking upon him, loved him and began to beseech him that he might be with him. And going out of the tomb they came into the house of the youth, for he was rich. And after six days, Jesus told him what to do, and in the evening, the youth came to him, wearing a linen cloth over his naked body. And he remained with him that night, for Jesus taught him the mystery of the Kingdom of God.'*

The American clinical psychologist Robert Kastenbaum stated that seeing an apple fall *upwards* (even but once) would be enough to convince us that Newton's Law of Universal Gravitation does not tell the whole story.

The analogy with what follows now may sound a bit tortuous, but the intention must be clear. The link between 'the presence of God or the Light' and an imprint of a human body – the apple that falls upwards – was indeed shown objectively and graphically in a British nursing home in 1981.

This is the highly publicized story of father Francis O'Leary, then head of St Joseph's Hospice in Thornton, near Liverpool.

On 27th of February of that year, the 44-year-old Les was admitted to the Hospice with terminal pancreatic carcinoma: the West Indian man had only ten more days to live. Despite his critical and depressing condition, the unschooled and unmarried Les, who was administered massive doses of painkillers, stayed remarkably courageous. His sweet and courteous character eased the difficult task of the personnel: being in Les's presence had even a quieting effect. He immediately asked for a Bible and, in passing, told a nurse that 'he had come here to meet God'.

A couple of days after his admittance, father O'Leary and a prayer group entered Les's room and asked if he wanted to pray with them. Les made no objection. What followed was a typical, culturally coloured deathbed vision, which is well documented in the parapsychological literature.

*'After a while,'* father O'Leary wrote, *'Les suddenly sat bolt upright, and looking towards the bottom of the bed, said, "Oh my Lord, you are here. You have come for me! But me, Les, have never done anything for you!" Then, looking at his hands, which were large for his size, he continued, "These hands have done nothing for you, and yet you have come to me."*

*We all left the room quietly, deeply moved by the spirituality of a person who himself had said that although brought up a Christian, he had not taken an active part in his faith during the latter years.'*

Les died shortly afterwards, at 5.55 in the morning. His body was washed and prepared. A nursing assistant immediately started cleaning the empty bed.

The scrubbing of the nylon mattress cover with a disinfectant turned out to be more difficult than expected. Surprised by the tenacity of some of the spots, the assistant suddenly noticed it was the imprint of a stretched left hand. On closer look, there were also contours visible of the posterior, an arm, a shoulder and even a part of the face. The staff members were assembled, and everybody could see with his and her own eyes the wonderful phenomenon.

Father O'Leary – who, being a preacher, did not exclude a miracle – took the mattress cover home but kept it for five years in a plastic bag. Only in 1986, after reading an article on the Turin Shroud, he decided to ask scientific advice about the image on the nylon cover.

The so called Jospice Imprint has been examined extensively, but no satisfying answers could be given as to the how, what and why of the image. Textile experts could not explain how the image had been produced on the nylon mattress protector that had lain underneath a – unaffected – cotton sheet.

The American Shroud expert Frederick Zugibe (see Chapter I) also studied the nylon cover. He took photographs, filmed, scanned and enlarged the ochre image with sophisticated equipment.

After an extensive analysis in his New York laboratory, Dr Zugibe concluded that the metabolite bilirubin in the very dark urine of Les (who had become incontinent) could have played a role in the formation of the imprint. But how this had happened exactly was far from clear.

Even though considerably less dramatic than the Turin Shroud – and on a number of points divergent from it – the Jospice Imprint up till now remains an equally unique enigma.

## Abba Sisoes

What did Les see that afternoon at the foot of his bed? Quite possible that it was the same lustrous white Light (invariably identified with God) from the countless deathbed visions testified in the parapsychological literature. But in the case of Les, this Universal Light exteriorized itself, for an inexplicable reason, in a hesychastic way, shortly before he died.

In father O'Leary's report we read that the night sister had come to move Les at 5.30. He died twenty-five minutes later; apparently he was alone. It is tempting to believe that, at that moment, the same thing happened to Les as what happened to the desert hermit Abba Sisoes shortly before he passed away.

The elderly and very pious Abba Sisoes was surrounded at his deathbed by his mourning disciples, and he complained of having shown so little repentance during his life. So he asked the angels and celestial creatures that had appeared in front of him, for some respite.

*'Suddenly,'* one reads in the 5$^{th}$ century *Sayings of the Fathers,* a collection of maxims of the Egyptian hermits, *'his face radiated like the sun and everyone around the bed was frightened. And he said to them: "Look! Look! The lord has come, and He says: Bring me the chosen instrument from the desert". And he passed away and became as the lightning, and the room was filled with a sweet aroma'...*

Monk Macarius of the Simonos-Petras monastery on Athos reported that a similar thing happened when father Augustin died. In 1965, mortally ill in his bed, this aged Russian hermit would call out almost every day:

*'The holy angels are coming there! There, do you not see them?'* and *'The saints are here! The holy Mother of God!'*

When Augustin finally passed away *'his face all of a sudden lightened up, dazzlingly, three times'*...

Does all this sound too fantastic to be true? In no way the previous cases are unique.

It even happened to the famous analytical psychologist Carl Gustav Jung!

Jung, whose mystic predisposition is well known, wrote in his autobiography *Memories, Dreams, Reflections* how in 1944 he suffered a life-threatening heart failure, lost consciousness and was transported to the hospital. There, he was the victim of overwhelming 'deliria and visions'. In other words, he had a near-death experience – long before the word and the phenomenon were popularized by the American NDE expert Dr Raymond Moody.

Jung described how his out-of-body experience offered him later a clear view of the planet earth from an estimated distance of 1500 km!

What is particularly interesting in this context are Jung's own words:

*'(...) The images were so tremendous that I concluded to myself that I was close to death. My nurse afterwards told me, "It was as if you were surrounded by a bright glow." That was a phenomenon she had sometimes observed in the dying, she added. I had reached the outermost limit, and do not know whether I was in a dream or an ecstasy'*...

In 2010 Dr Moody published another book that was as groundbreaking as his bestseller *Life after Life* from

1975. This time Moody reported on *SDE's* or *Shared Death Experiences*, his, with numerous examples illustrated, research on the transcendental experiences of family members and friends, at the deathbed of their loved ones.

An SDE refers to the sudden mental *participation* of a healthy visitor in the classical deathbed visions of a dying person, the NDE-like phase that he is allegedly experiencing at the moment of his death. Suddenly, and to his amazement, the visitor momentarily takes part in the transcendental experience, witnesses the overwhelming Light, sees deceased relatives, etc...

**Icon**
The baptism with the 'Light of the Kingdom of God', that had always been an elitist affair, had become a very rare practice at the beginning of the second millennium. Only a few initiated and persevering Hesychasts were still capable of fully experiencing it. It is my hypothesis, that a traditional, secret ritual with a shroud over a naked face or body was still practised by them.

Admittedly, all this sounds very unreal and more like a fairy tale. But we cannot ignore the observable, tangible, yet still inapprehensible Turin Shroud: something happened here that verges on the supernatural...

It is not a coincidence that the Hesychasts attributed a special significance to the *icon* phenomenon. The painting of icons was indeed a particularly important activity for the Hesychast (August 6, the annual celebration of the *Metamorphosis* is also the high day of the icon painters.) Between the 13<sup>th</sup> and 16<sup>th</sup> century, they produced the most remarkable examples.

Through an ascetic lifestyle (fasting, praying, mortification), the Hesychast attempted to transfer the 'holy energy' of God's force to the painted representation of a saint. In the icon theology, the painted saint is thus literally transfigured. And visible as such to the eyes. Adoration of an icon of Christ then has nothing to do with sacrilege. The transfigured portrait is, by virtue of the Hesychast painting technique, not an image, but of divine nature.

The oldest icon form and its prototype is the so called *Acheiropoietos,* or the portrait of Christ 'that is not made by human hands'. It is thought to represent, invariably, a 'copy' of the legendary portrait of Jesus, given to the leprous King Abgar V of Edessa. Ian Wilson has erroneously hypothesized that Abgar's 'irradiated' and healing relic was conserved and later recovered as the Turin Shroud.

*'He is the reflection of God's glory and the exact imprint of God's very being,'* is written in Hebrews 1:3.

And in Colossians 1:15 we read:

*'He is the image* (eikon) *of the invisible God, the firstborn of all creation.'*

These verses refer to the glorified Jesus Christ, the second Adam of before the Fall, created as God's image (or ignited by God's Light). But these verses could just as well refer to a 'transfigured' Hesychast, or to the man on the Turin Shroud.

*'As many of you, as were baptized into Christ, have clothed yourselves with Christ,'* is written by Paul (Galatians 3:27).

And so, one could regard the *personal* imprint of a 14th century Hesychast 'baptized into Christ' as the perfect, and most literal form of an *Acheiropoietos*...

The so called Turin Shroud belongs, strictly speaking, to the Eastern Orthodox Church: it is the sublime product of the Hesychast spirituality and theology. Through his greedy Latin family in Greece, Geoffrey of Charny acquired this extraordinary linen.

We can imagine the cloth was a compelling piece of evidence in the council on the Hesychast issue in 1341. Brought back from Constantinople, it was preserved in a Greek monastery, eventually stolen, and taken to France.

Although for an Orthodox monk, the most direct way to Christ's Glory is one of extreme austerity and deliberate suffering, I do not want to make a link with the dreadful signs of violence on the Turin Shroud. The Eastern Orthodox Shroud was first shown in the 14th century; it was the moment that the Black Death (the Plague) pandemic raged all over Europe, and when the gory, heretic flagellant confraternities became very popular in large parts of Roman Catholic territory.

It is probable that Jesus' 'wounds of passion' were painted on the Shroud *after* its hesychastic creation, aiming to emphasize his deification. Possibly the linen was 'retouched' – by the alleged forger to whom Bishop Pierre d'Arcis was referring to in 1389? – with pigment, with animal blood, or even with human blood, to increase the fascinating appearance of the lucrative relic.

No wonder the very devout Charny family was convinced to possess the genuine burial Shroud of Jesus the Nazorean...

# REFERENCES

## I. The Turin Shroud

P.E. Damon, M.S. Tite et al, *Radiocarbon dating of the Shroud of Turin.* Nature, vol. 337, 16-2, 1989.

R.E.M. Hedges et al, *Radiocarbon dates from the Oxford AMS system: Archaeometry date list 11.* Archaeometry, 1990, 32, p. 233.

Ian Wilson, *The Turin Shroud.* Penguin Books, England, 1979.

Ian Wilson, *The Blood and the Shroud.* Orion, London, 1998.

Christopher Knight and Robert Lomas, *The Second Messiah: Templars, The Turin Shroud, and the Great Secret of Freemasonry.* Barnes & Noble Books, New York, 2000.

Remi Van Haelst, *Het gelaat van Kristus – De Lijkwade van Turijn.* Uitgave N.V. De Vlijt, 1986 (Dutch).

Gilbert Lavoie, *Unlocking the Secrets of the Shroud.* Thomas More Press, Allen, Texas, 1998.

Rodney Hoare, *The Testimony of the Shroud.* Quarterbook, London, 1978.

H. Kersten en E.R. Gruber, *Das Jesus komplott*. Langen Muller, München, 1992 (German).

Raymond N. Rogers, *Studies on the radiocarbon sample from the Shroud of Turin*. Thermochimica Acta, Vol. 425, Issues 1-2, Jan. 20, 2005.

V. Miller en D. Lynn, *De lijkwade van Turijn*. Natuur & Techniek, 60, 10, 1992 (Dutch).

Oreste Favaro, *The Holy Shroud in the light of the Gospels and of modern science – The Way of the Cross*. Torino, 1978.

Jack Markwardt, *Was the Shroud in Languedoc during the missing years?*
- http://www.shroud.com/markward.htm

F.T. Zugibe, *Pierre Barbet Revisited*,
- http://www.shroud.com/zugibe.htm

Antonio Lombatti, *Doubt concerning the coins over the eyes*,
- http://www.shroud.com/lombatti.htm

Gary Vikan, *Debunking the Shroud: Made by human hands*,
- http://www.shroud.com/bar.htm

Isabel Piczek, *Is the Shroud of Turin a painting?*
- http://www.shroud.com/piczek.htm

Barrie M. Schwortz, *Is the Shroud of Turin a medieval photograph?*
- http://www.shroud.com/pdfs/orvieto.pdf

David Ford, *The Shroud of Turin's 'Blood' Images: Blood, or Paint?*
- http://www.shroud.com/papers.htm

A.D. Accetta et al, *Nuclear medicine and its relevance to the Shroud of Turin*,
- http://www.shroud.com/pdfs/accett2.pdf

## II. Powerful Works

G.H. Moreno et al., *Comparative study of the sudarium of Oviedo and the Shroud of Turin,* 1998.

Burton L. Mack, *The Lost Gospel: The Book of Q & Christian Origins.* Harper Collins, 1993.

Charlotte Allen, *The Search for a no-frills Jesus.* The Atlantic Monthly, Dec. 1996.

Drs. Gijs van den Brink, *De hermeneutiek van de schriftgeleerden en apostelen* (Dutch),
- http://www.elim.nl/ned/nt/hermapos.htm

David T. Runia, *Philo of Alexandria and the Beginnings of Christian Thought,*
- www.torreys.org/philo-art/philo&beg.html

*Book of Enoch,*
- http://www.reluctant-messenger.com/enoch.htm

W.H.C. Tenhaeff, *Oorlogsvoorspellingen. Een onderzoek met betrekking tot proscopie in verband met het wereldgebeuren.* H.P. Leopold, Den Haag, 1948 (Dutch).

Dr H. Somers, *Jezus de Messias – Was het christendom een vergissing?* Uitg. Epo, Antwerpen, 1987 (Dutch).

G. Zorab, *Het opstandingsverhaal in het licht der parapsychologie.* H.P. Leopold, Den Haag, 1949 (Dutch).

Jon Klimo, *Channeling: Investigations on Receiving Information from Paranormal Sources.* Los Angeles, CA: Jeremy P. Tarcher, 1987.

*Insight on the Scriptures.* Watchtower Bible and Tract Society of New York. Inc., Intern. Bible Students Association. Brooklyn, N.Y., 1995, 1997.

*The Kingdom Interlinear Translation of the Greek Scriptures.* Watchtower Bible and Tract Society of New York. Inc., Intern. Bible Students Association. Brooklyn, N.Y., 1969.
Jewish Encyclopedia. Com

The Scripture quotations contained herein are from the **New Revised Standard Version Bible**, copyright © 1989, by the Division of Christian Education of the National Council of the Churches of Christ in the U.S.A., and are used by permission. All rights reserved.

## III. Death and Resurrection

Esther A. de Boer, *Mary Magdalene beyond the Myth.* SCM Press, London, 1997.
Dr A.L.S. Bär, *Paulus, rationalist en mysticus.* Servire, Wassenaar, 1972 (Dutch).
S.G.F. Brandon, *Religion in ancient history: Studies in ideas, men and events.* George Allen and Unwin, London 1973.
Graham Lester, *Paul and the mission to the Gentiles: a study in the history of scholarship.* 1998,
- http://people.delphiforums.com/tglit/graham/Paul.html
Daniel Wojcik, *All rise!* Fortean Times 129, December 1999, p.46.
J. G. Sutherland, *De Bijbel en de Antieke Mysteriën.* Servire, Wassenaar, 1975 (Dutch).
R.E. Witt, *Isis in the Graeco-Roman world.* Thames and Hudson, London, 1971.

Paul Foucart, *Les Mystères d'Eleusis.* Aug. Picard, Paris, 1914. Heruitgave in 1992 door Pardès, Puiseaux, France (French).

Victor Magnien, *Les Mystères d'Eleusis.* Payot, Paris, 1929 (French).

G. Méautis, *Les dieux de la Grèce et les Mystères d'Eleusis.* P.U.F., Paris, 1959 (French).

Kalliope Preka-Alexandri, *Eleusis.* Ministry of Culture, Archaeological Receipts Fund, Athens 1991.

*Homeric Hymn to Demeter,*

- http://www.uh.edu/~cldue/texts/demeter.html

R. Gordon Wasson et al., *Persephone's Quest: Entheogens and the Origins of Religion.* Yale University Press, New Haven/London, 1986.

R. Gordon Wasson et al., *The Road to Eleusis: Unveiling the Secret of the Mysteries.* Harcourt Brace Jovanovich, 1978.

H.P. Blavatsky, *Isis Unveiled: A Master-Key to the Mysteries of Ancient and Modern Science and Theology.* Pasadena, CA: Theosophical University Press, 1999.

Joscelyn Godwin, *Mystery Religions in the Ancient World.* Thames and Hudson, London, 1981.

Apuleius; Kenney, E.J. (Trans.) *The Golden Ass.* Penguin, London, 1998, rev. 2004.

*Dialogues of Plato,*

- https://www.ellopos.net/elpenor/greek-texts/ancient-greece/plato/default.asp

The Scripture quotations contained herein are from the **New Revised Standard Version Bible,** copyright © 1989, by the Division of Christian Education of the

National Council of the Churches of Christ in the U.S.A., and are used by permission. All rights reserved.

## IV. The Near-Death Experience

Paul Brunton, *A Search in Secret Egypt.* Barnes and Noble, New York, 2002.

Raymond Moody, *Life After Life.* Bantam, New York, 1975.

Susan J. Blackmore, *Beyond the Body. An Investigation of Out-of-the-Body Experiences.* Heinemann, London, 1982.

S. Muldoon & H. Carrington, *The Projection of the Astral Body.* Rider & Company, London, 1968.

Kenneth Ring, *From Alpha to Omega: Ancient Mysteries and the Near-Death Experience.* Anabiosis, Vol.5, No. 2, 1987.

Michael Grosso, *Self, Eternity and the Mysteries: A Speculative Response to Kenneth Ring's Paper.* Anabiosis-The Journal for Near-Death Studies, Vol. 4, No. 2, 1984.

Red. Evelyne-Sarah Mercie, *La Mort Transfigurée. Recherches sur les expériences vécues aux approches de la mort.* IANDS-France. L'Age du verseau, Paris, 1992 (French).

Pim van Lommel et al, *Near Death experience in survivors of cardiac arrest: a prospective study in the Netherlands.* The Lancet, Vol 358, December 15, 2001.

Kenneth Ring, Sharon Cooper, *Mindsight: Near-Death and Out-of-Body Experiences in the Blind.* Palo Alto, CA: William James Center for Consciousness Studies, Institute of Transpersonal Psychology, 1999.

Karl L.R. Jansen, *The Ketamine Model of the Near Death Experience: A central Role for the NMDA Receptor.*
- http://leda.lycaeum.org/ Documents/
Karl L.R. Jansen, *Ketamine (K) and Quantum Psychiatry.* Asylum 11 (3) 19-21, 1999.
Wilder Penfield, The *role of the temporal cortex in certain psychical phenomena.* The Journal of Mental Science, Vol 101, July 1955.
Hans Plomp, *Ervaringsaspecten van ketamine.* PAN-forum, nulnummer, mei 1995 (Dutch).
Richard Wilhelm/C.G. Jung, *The Secret of the Golden Flower: a Chinese Book of Life.* Kegan Paul, Trench Trubner & Co, London, 1932.


## V. The holy spirit

Viscount Adare, *Experiences in spiritualism with Mr D. D. Home.* Imprint: Arno Press, New York, 1976.
P. Gaultier Briand O.F.M., *Nazareth Judeo-Chrétienne.* Franciscan Printing Press, Jerusalem (French).
Marcel Simon, *De joodse sekten ten tijde van Jezus.* W. ten Have N.V., Amsterdam, 1965 (Dutch).
Mircea Eliade, *Rites and Symbols of Initiation.* Harper & Row, New York, 1975.
Philippe Roy, *Le Consolament Cathare.* Ed. Dervy, Paris, 1996 (French).
*The Hymn of the Pearl - The Acts of Thomas,*
- http://gnosis.org/library/hymnpearl.htm
*Secret Mark,*
- http://www.earlychristianwritings.com/secretmark.html.

- *Gospel of Peter,*
http://www.earlychristianwritings.com/Gospelpeter.html

The Scripture quotations contained herein are from the **New Revised Standard Version Bible,** copyright © 1989, by the Division of Christian Education of the National Council of the Churches of Christ in the U.S.A., and are used by permission. All rights reserved.

## VI. The Light Body

J.J. Poortman, *Vehicles of Consciousness. I, II, III, IV.* The Theosophical Society in the Netherlands, Utrecht 1978.

*The weird science database of Electric People,*
- http://www.amasci.com/weird/unusual/zap.html

J.J. van Hemmen, *Biologisch licht.* Natuur en Techniek, 42, 8, 1974 (Dutch).

S. Ostrander and L. Schroeder, *Psychic Discoveries Behind the Iron Curtain.* Bantam, New York, 1970.

Min Zhao et al, *Electrical signals control wound healing through phosphatidylinositol-3-OH kinase-big gamma and PTEN.* Nature 27 July 2006 (vol. 442), p. 457-60.

B. W. Chwirot, *Ultra-weak luminescence as a source of information on biological systems,*
- http://www.datadiwan.de/iib/ib0601e_.htm

Colin Wilson, *Poltergeist! A study in destructive haunting.* Caxton Editions, London, 2000.

Larry E. Arnold, *Ablaze! The mysterious fires of spontaneous human combustion.* M. Evans & Co., New York, 1995.

John E. Heymer, *The Entrancing Flame*. Little, Brown & Co., 1996.

Herbert Thurston s.j., *The Physical Phenomena of Mysticism*. Roman Catholic Books, 2007.

Walter Nigg, *Great Saints*. Aldor, 1948.

Dr Melvin Morse and Paul Perry, *Closer to the light: Learning from children's near-death experiences*. Villard, New York, 1990.

Bob Rickard, *Doctor Near-Death?* Fortean Times 294, November 2012.

Br. Arni Decorte, *Padre Pio. Herinneringen aan een begenadigde getuige van Christus*. Bierbeek, 1987 (Dutch).

Antoine Imbert-Gourbeyre, *La stigmatisation (1894)*. Ed. Jérôme Millon, 1996 (French).

Edward F. Kelly et al, *Irreducible Mind*. Rowman & Littlefield, UK, 2007.

The Scripture quotations contained herein are from the **New Revised Standard Version Bible,** copyright © 1989, by the Division of Christian Education of the National Council of the Churches of Christ in the U.S.A., and are used by permission. All rights reserved.

### VII. Kundalini

Lee Sannella, *The Kundalini Experience: Psychosis or Transcendence?* Lower Lake, CA: Integral Publishing, 1987.

J.-P. Jourdan, *NDE and transcendental experiences*. Journal of Near Death Studies, vol. 12, nr. 3, Spring 1994.

Hubert Larcher in *La Mort Transfigurée. Recherches sur les expériences vécues aux approches de la mort.* Deel 6. IANDS-France. L'Age du verseau, Paris, 1992 (French).

Adrian Jackson interviews Dr Hiroshi Motoyama,
- http://www.shareintl.org/archives/health-healing/hh_adjenergetic.html

Gopi Krishna, *Kundalini: The Evolutionary Energy in Man.* Shambala Publications, London, 1997.

Frits Staal, *Exploring Mysticism: A Methodological Essay.* University of California Press, 1975.

Kenneth Ring, *Near-Death and UFO Encounters As Shamanic Initiations: Some Conceptual and Evolutionary Implications.* ReVision, Vol. 11, No. 3, Winter 1989.

Mary Lutyens, *Krishnamurti: 1. The Years of Awakening, 2. The Years of Fulfilment, 3. The Open Door.* Avon Books, New York, 1991.

Pupul Jayakar, *Krishnamurti: A Biography.* Harper & Row, Publishers, 1986.

*Krishnamurti over Krishnamurti.* Uitg. Synthese, Amsterdam, 2004 (Dutch).

Radha Rajagopal-Sloss, *Lives in the Shadow with J. Krishnamurti.* Bloomsbury, 1991.

## VIII. The Hesychasts

Alexander Golitzin, *The Living Witness of the Holy Mountain.* St. Tikhon's Seminary Press, Pennsylvania, 1999.

Jean Biès, *Athos, La Montagne transfigurée.* Les Deux Océans, Paris, 1997 (French).

Jean-Yves Leloup, *Écrits sur l'Hésychasme. Une tradition contemplative oubliée.* Albin Michel, Paris, 1990 (French).

*La Philocalie* (French),
- http://livres-mystiques.com/partieTEXTES/Philocalie/table.html

K. Rasmussen, *Intellectual Culture of the Iglulik Eskimos, "Report of the 5th Thule Expedition 1921-24" VII, n° 1.* Copenhague, 1929.

J.-P. Jourdan, *NDE and transcendental experiences.* Journal of Near Death Studies, vol. 12, nr. 3, Spring 1994.

John S. Romanides, *Notes on the Palamite Controversy and related topics.* The Greek Orthodox Theological Review, Vol. VI, nr. 2, Winter 1960-'61 and Vol. IX, nr. 2, Winter 1963-'64.

Raynor C. Johnson, *The Imprisoned Splendor.* Hodder & Stoughton, London, 1953.


### IX. The Athos Shroud

Nicholaos Economidis, *The History of Mount Athos During the Byzantine Age.*
- www.culture.gr/2/21/218/e21811.html

Daniel C. Scavone, *Evidence for the Shroud in Constantinopel prior tot 1204,*
- http://www.shroud.com/pdfs/scavone.pdf

*St. Seraphim of Sarov's Conversation With Nicholas Motovilov,*

Séraphim de Sarov, *L'Entretien avec Motovilov.* Éditions Arfuyen, 2002 (French).
- http://orthodoxinfo.com/praxis/wonderful.aspx

A.D. Accetta, K. Lyons, J. Jackson, *Nuclear medicine and its relevance to the Turin Shroud,*
- http://www.shroud.com/pdfs/accett2.pdf

Bernard A. Power, *Image formation on the Holy Shroud of Turin by attenuation of radiation in air.* Collegamento pro Sindone, Maart 2002.

Régis en Brigitte Dutheil in *La Mort Transfigurée. Recherches sur les expériences vécues aux approches de la mort.* Deel 3. IANDS-France. L'Age du verseau, Paris, 1992 (French).

Peter Carr, *The Imprint,*
- http://www.shroud.com/pdfs/imprint.pdf

F.T. Zugibe, *The Jospice Mattress Cover Image,*
- http://www.shroud.com/pdfs/mattress.pdf

Jung, C.G., *Memories, Dreams, Reflections.* HarperCollins Publishers, 1989.

E. A. Wallis Budge transl., *The Paradise of the Holy Fathers, vol II.* St. Nactarios Press, Seattle, 1984.

Raymond Moody, *Glimpses of Eternity. An Investigation into Shared Death Experiences.* Rider, London, 2010.

John Brentnall, *The language of Orthodox icons,*
- http://www.farmington.ac.uk/documents/old_docs/Brentnall.htm

# INDEX

A

Abba Sisoes, 44, 166, 211,
Abgar V, King, 18, 200, 214,
Accetta, August D., 205, 218, 228,
Acheiropoietos, 19, 214, 215,
Actions of Pilate, 23, 39, 48, 71, 128, 185,
Acts of Thomas, 48, 113, 114, 117, 118, 121, 223,
Adare, Lord, 114, 223,
Adler, Alan, 31,
Agio Oros, 196,
Agnes de Charpigny, 198,
Alexander the Great, 42, 105, 137, 149, 226,
Allen, Nicholas, 32, 33, 217, 219, 220,
Amanita muscaria, 86,
Anaktoron, 83, 84, 89, 106,
anchorites, 178, 188, 195, 196,

Andronicus III, Emperor, 188, 189, 190,
angel, 73, 93, 119, 120, 121, 187
Antisthenes, 41
Antonacci, Mark, 27
Apostle Philip, 17, 27, 52, 63, 69, 70, 78, 104
106, 114, 116, 130, 146, 153,
Apostles, 148, 65, 67, 68, 105, 114, 115, 125, 170
180, 191, 192, 193
Applewhite, Marshall, 71
Arcis, Pierre d', 14, 15, 215
Arnold, Larry E., 142, 224
Ascension of Isaiah, 17, 113, 120, 166, 180
astral projection, 86, 94, 95, 96, 97, 104, 133
134, 135, 166, 222
Aua, shaman, 184
aura, 19, 134, 144, 172

229

## B

Baan, Bastiaan, 136,
Baden, Michael, 30
Ball, Philip, 29, 162
Ballestrero, Archbishop, 34
Baphomet, 20
baptism, 111, 115, 117-121, 124, 127-129, 131, 191, 201, 208, 213
baptism with water, 115, 118, 131
Bär, A.L.S., 66, 220
Barbet, Pierre, 22-24, 218
Barlaam, 188-190
Barth, Karl, 66
Basil II, Emperor, 195, 196
Bentov, Itzhak, 165
biofield, 145, 146, 148, 166
biological plasma body, 101, 133, 142, 144, 145, 147, 148, 170, 171, 224
bioluminescence, 147, 148, 149
bio-oscillators, 165
biophotons, 148
bioplasma, 145, 146
bioplastic coating, 35
Blachernae, Church of St Mary of, 19, 198
Blackmore, Susan, 94, 97, 98, 100, 222
Blavatsky, H.P., 85, 86, 134, 166, 181, 221
Books of Wisdom, 49, 94, 96, 111, 190, 217, 225
Bozzano, Ernesto, 194
Brigitte Dutheil, 206, 207, 228
Brunton, Paul, 91, 92, 93, 103, 222
Bucklin, Robert, 117
Bultmann, Rudolf, 66
Byzantine Church, 178

## C

Caes, Danny, 138
Capernaum, paralytic of, 77
carbon-14, 9, 12, 34, 35, 198
Cathars, 20, 119-121, 135
chakra, 160
Chalcidice, peninsula, 195
Charny, de, 14, 15, 20, 198
Christian theology, 55, 62, 64
Christians, 19, 20, 50, 52, 66, 68, 70, 116, 124, 155
Church of St. Mary of Blachernae, 198
Clari, Robert de, 19
Clement of Alexandria, 182, 80, 87, 122, 126
Colin Wilson, 224, 142
Committee for Skeptical Inquiry, 29, 94

Comnenus, Theodore Angelus, 199
Consolamentum, 121
cripple at the pool of Beth-Zatha, 128
Crossan, John Dominic, 41
crucifixion, 23, 66, 67, 78, 154
CSI, 94
Cynics, 41, 42
Cyril of Jerusalem, 192, 118

D

Damascus, 17, 18, 68, 78, 105
Danin, Avinoam, 26
Demeter, 79, 81, 83, 87, 221
Deutero-Isaiah, 60
diamond body, 108, 135
Dijck, Leonie van den, 152
Diogenes of Sinope, 41
double, 16, 32, 94, 104, 117, 134, 145, 160
doxa, 115
du Teil, Joseph, 198
dynamin, 39, 114, 130

E

early Christians, 66, 116
Eastern-Orthodox, 18
Ebionites, 117
Edessa, 17-20, 198, 200, 214,

Egyptian Book of the Dead, 103
electromagnetic phenomena, 133
Eleusinian, 81, 84, 89
Eleusinian Mysteries, 79, 80, 86, 106, 122, 126
Eleusis, 79, 80, 84, 87, 107, 221
Elijah, 61, 72, 73, 75
Emmaus, 68
Enoch, 55, 56
Enrie, Guiseppe, 21, 22
entheogen, 86
epitaphioi threnoi, 19
epopteia, 84, 85, 106, 107, 181
Essenes, 58, 65, 78, 119
Eusebius, 18, 116
Evangelists, 37, 38, 40, 48, 49, 55, 67
extrasensory perception, 96, 141
Ezekiel, 55

F

Filas, Francis, 25
fire, 31, 56, 59, 60, 75, 84, 89, 106, 107, 109, 113, 115, 117, 118, 124, 127, 128, 129, 135, 138, 142, 143, 147, 150, 153, 161, 162-164, 183, 185, 186,

197, 199, 208, 16
flash photolysis, 26
force, 25, 39, 74, 103, 112-114, 130, 133, 137, 142, 159, 160, 164, 166, 170-175, 179, 182, 189, 192, 193, 204, 214,
Fortean Times, 70, 220, 225
Fourth Crusade, 197, 198, 19
Fox, Oliver, 96, 97
Francis of Assisi, 154
Frei, Max, 24, 29

### G

Galilee, 12, 38, 40, 41, 44, 45, 47, 67, 201
Garden of Gethsemane, 74
Garza-Valdès, Leoncio, 34
Gentiles, 52, 63, 69, 78, 106
Gionella, Luigi, 34
Giuseppe Costa, Giuseppe, 194
Glaucos, 83
Gnostic, 19, 43, 46, 72, 107, 120-122, 126, 135
God's Kingdom, 62, 88, 128, 129, 191, 192
Golden Dawn, 95
Golden Flower, 107-109, 135, 136
Gospel, 14, 17, 37, 42, 43, 46, 47, 49, 67, 120, 122-126, 130, 139, 208
Gospel of Thomas, 17, 43
grain, 78, 106
Great Pyramid of Giza, 91
Greek canon, 120
Grosso, Michael, 103, 171
Gruber, E.R., 35
Gurwitsch, Alexander, 137, 149

### H

Habermas, Gary, 43
hallucinogenic, 86
Heaven's Gate, 70
Hebrew Bible, 40, 60, 61
Hellenistic, 39, 52, 54, 62, 68, 72, 78, 80, 105, 106, 116
Heller, John, 31
Heraclitus of Ephesus, 54
hermits, 182, 195, 196, 211
Hesychasm, 201, 163, 178, 179, 181, 188
Hesychast Controversy, 197, 190
Hesychia, 178
hiera, 83
Hierophant, 80, 83, 85, 89, 103, 107
Hierotheos Vlachos, Orthodox Archbishop, 192
Hippolytus, 106, 107
Hofmann, 86

holy spirit, 64, 65, 111-115, 117-119, 121, 124, 127, 128, 139, 143, 144, 164, 170, 180, 184, 191, 201-204
Home, Daniel Dungl, 114
Homer, 79, 83
Hugh de Lille Charpigny, 198
Human Batteries, 140-142, 161

I

IANDS, 93, 103
icon, 19, 213, 214
iconoclasm, 195
identical replication, 200
Iglulik Eskimos, 163
imagination, 97, 99, 108, 181
Imbert-Gourbeyre, Antoine, 156
initiation, 78-85, 87, 89, 105, 106, 118, 124, 127, 128, 181
Innocentius III, Pope, 199
International Association for Near-Death Studies, 93

J

Jackson, John P., 25
Jairus, daughter of, 74
James, M.R., 121
Jansen, Karl L.R., 99

Jehovah's Witnesses, 113
Jesus, 9, 12-15, 17, 18, 20, 22, 24, 31, 37-58, 60-78, 82, 85, 88, 105, 106, 108, 109, 114-120, 123-133, 135, 136, 138, 139, 145, 146, 154, 159, 166, 175-180, 187, 191-193, 198-202, 204, 208, 214, 215,
Jewish Antiquities, 39, 58
Jewish theology, 47, 62
John the Baptist, 16, 48, 49, 117, 118, 191
John Tsimiskis, Emperor, 196
John XIV Kalekas, 189
Johnson, Ken, 145
Joseph of Arimathea, 130
Josephus, Flavius, 39, 58, 63
Jospice Imprint, 210
Jourdan, Jean-Pierre, 163
Jumper, Eric J., 25
Jung, Carl Gustav, 212, 107

K

Kabod, 115
Karpokratians, 122
Kastenbaum, Robert, 208
Kersten, H., 35
ketamine, 99, 100
Kingdom of God', 45, 46, 61, 71, 72, 77, 105, 123, 124, 131, 191, 201, 204, 208, 213

Kirlian, Semyon and Valentina, 144
Knight, Christopher, 20
Knights Templar, 20
Krishna, Gopi, 167, 169, 170, 171
Krishnamurti, Jiddu, 172, 173, 202
Kundalini, 159-173, 207

L

Labouré, Catherine, 152
Lambertini, Prospero, 150
Larcher, Hubert, 171
laser, 26, 137
Lateau, Louise, 154
Lavoie, Gilbert 31
Lavra, 196
Leadbeater, C.W., 172
light, 18, 23, 26, 32, 33, 45, 47, 55, 58, 66, 68, 69, 71, 73, 75, 77, 78, 81, 83, 84, 87-89, 91, 93, 100, 103-106, 108, 115, 119, 120, 121, 127, 128, 133, 134, 135, 137, 138-144, 150-159, 162-164, 166, 168, 169, 171, 172, 179, 180-189, 190-194, 197, 200, 201-204, 206-208, 211, 213, 214
Light body, 120, 121, 135
Lindsay, Lord, 114
Lirey, 14, 198, 199
Logos, 54, 109
Lomas, Robert, 20
Lombatti, A, 26
Lommel, Pim, 101, 103
Los Alamos National Laboratory, 11
Louis I, Duke of Savoy, 15
LSD, 86
Lü Yen, 107, 109
luminous, 68, 72, 74, 115, 134, 149, 152, 162, 171, 185, 194, 204
Lusignan, Anne de, 15

M

Mack, Burton, 43
Maillard, 28
Maillard reaction, 28
Makhlouf, Charbel, 152
Mandylion, 18, 19, 198
Manicheans, 119, 121
Markward, Jack, 19
Mary Magdalene, 67, 74, 76, 125
Mashiach, 40, 54
McCrone, Walter C., 30
McElroy, William D., 147
Messiah, 40, 46-48, 50, 54-58, 60, 61, 65, 78, 116
metamorphosis, 45, 56, 74,

146, 179, 213
metanoia, 181, 189
Michael VIII Palaeologus, Emperor, 197
microwave radiation, 205
Miracle Worker, 12, 42, 50, 52, 128, 131, 203, 204
Molay, Jacques de, 20
Monaro, Anna, 149, 192
Monroe, Robert, 96
Moody, Raymond, 92, 95
Morse, Melvin, 100, 153, 193, 207
Moses, 54, 61, 72, 73, 75, 138
Moss, Thelma, 145
Motovilov, Nicolas, 202
Motoyama, Hiroshi, 165
Mount Athos, 178, 179, 192
Mount of Olives, 63, 67, 113, 125, 129
Mount Sinai, 75, 138, 178
Muldoon, Sylvan, 96
Mysteries, 78-88, 91, 101, 103-106, 118, 119, 122, 123, 126-128, 181, 201, 207
Mystery Cults, 79

N

Naassene, 107
Nain, young man of, 74
Nazorean, 14, 17, 18, 37, 52, 55, 63, 66, 68, 71, 116, 119, 127, 133, 139, 146, 172, 187, 191-193, 198, 200, 204, 215
Nazoreans, 117
NDE, 83, 87, 91-95, 98-104, 153, 163, 171, 207, 212, 213
near-death experiences, 91, 93, 103, 134, 225
Nestorians, 109
New Testament, 41, 48, 52, 63-65, 70, 112, 115, 120, 134, 146, 164, 182
Nickell, Joe, 29
Nicodemus, 130, 131
Notowitch, Nicolos, 159
noûs, 181, 192
numinous, 72, 79, 104, 126, 163, 178, 186, 192

O

O'Leary, Francis, 208
OBE, 95-97
Old Testament, 40, 45, 48, 49, 55, 64, 112, 115, 120, 164
Orthodox, 18-20, 62, 122, 152, 178-181, 188, 190, 192, 197, 201, 202, 204, 205, 215
Osis, Karl, 95
Osty, 59
out-of-body experience, 93-95, 98, 99, 103, 104, 134, 212, 222

## P

Palamas, Gregory, 188-191, 192
parakletos, 113, 121
Paul, 21, 24, 48, 52-54, 63-65, 68-72, 75-78, 91-93, 103-105, 108, 111, 114, 116, 117, 128, 146, 153, 187, 201, 214
Paulicians, 19
Pauline gifts, 181
Penfield, Wilder, 100
Pentecost, 113, 114, 170
Pernoud, Régine, 10
personal Ego, 85, 92, 181
pesher, 48
Peter, 54, 57, 68, 72, 111, 113, 115-117, 125, 130, 191, 201
Pharisee, 64, 65, 68, 119, 130
Phillips, Thomas J., 27
Philo, 54, 55
physical body, 70, 71, 74-77, 92, 93, 96, 104, 106, 111, 119-121, 135, 146, 155, 160, 173, 179, 180, 189, 192
physiological pneuma, 134
Pia, Secondo, 21
Picknett, Lynn, 32
Piczek, Isabel, 30
Pilate, 39, 66, 130
Pio, Padre, 153, 154
Plato, 54, 84, 87, 189
Plomp, Hans, 101
Plotinus, 87, 88, 106, 126, 128
Plutarch, 81, 82, 84, 187
pneuma agion, 111, 112, 180, 201
Ponce de la Roche, 199
Poor Clair Nuns, 16
Poortman, J.J., 133, 146
Pope Francis, 15, 38
Power, Bernard, 206
prana, 164, 166, 171
Prayer of the Heart, 180
precognition, 58, 59, 93
preternatural phenomenon, 10
Prince, Clive, 32
Proclus, 87
prophet, 40, 45, 50, 55, 73, 75, 120
prophets, 40, 45, 54, 57, 64, 112, 117
Protti, Giocondo, 149
psychedelic, 86, 94, 157, 169
psychic pneuma, 134
psychobiophysical, 36, 38, 47, 49, 57, 58, 99, 127, 160-163, 170, 171, 176-178

## Q

quameneq, 163, 184
Quelle, 42, 43

## R

Rabboni., 61
radiocarbon, 36
radiocarbon dating, 9, 12, 33, 34, 177, 200, 204
Raes, Gilbert, 24
rapture, 69-71
Realino, Bernardino, 151
Reanimation, 28, 92, 102, 103
Régis Dutheil, 206
resurrection, 27, 38, 39, 60, 63, 64-66, 68-73, 76-79, 105, 106, 111, 113, 115, 116, 124, 127-129, 132, 134-136, 159, 179, 193, 199, 201, 204
resuscitate, 76, 104, 106, 129, 136
Rig Veda, 86, 144
Rinaudo, Jean-Baptiste, 27, 35
Ring, Kenneth, 103, 171
Rogers, Raymond R., 26
Roman, 23, 25, 37, 40, 41, 50, 52, 56, 57, 62, 63, 66, 78-80, 91, 130, 131, 197, 201
Roman-Catholics, 38, 79, 112, 116, 117, 126, 178, 179, 188, 190, 191, 215
Romanos I Lecapenos, Emperor, 195
Rosencreutz, Christian, 136
Rosicrucian Order, 136
ruah, 112, 115, 134, 164
Rubik, Beverly, 148, 166
Ruck, Carl A.P., 86

## S

Sadducees, 64, 119
Sainte Chapelle, Chambéry, 16
Sannella, Lee, 162, 165
Scaravelli, Vanda, 175
Scavone, Daniel S., 19, 199
Schafersman, Steven D., 29
Schiedam, Lidwina of, 152
Schwortz, Barrie, 32, 33, 36
Seliger, Howard H., 147
semeia, 43
Seraphim of Sarov, 203, 204
Shared Death Experiences, 213
Shekinah, 115, 179
Sheldrake, Rupert, 145
shining, 56, 73, 75, 83, 84, 109, 134, 145, 194
Shroud of Turin Research Project (STURP), 29, 32
siddhis, 163, 181
Silvanus, Abba, 186
sindona, 37, 123, 125
Skeptic, 29, 66, 89, 97, 99, 156, 177, 193
skeptics, 68, 94, 99, 137, 142, 145, 152, 199

Smith, Morton, 122, 124
soma pneumatikon, 76
soma psychikon, 76
soma tes doxes., 115
Son of Man, 49, 55-57, 60, 61, 77, 78, 106, 193
Sophia, 18, 49, 78, 189
Sophocles, 82
Soubirous, Bernadette, 151
soudarion, 37
Spirit gifts, 114, 121
spiritual body, 75, 76, 106, 121
Spiritual Ego, 85, 88, 181
Spontaneous human combustion, 142
Staal, Frits, 166
Steiner, Rudolf, 136
Stephan III, Pope, 200
stigmata, 15, 154, 155, 157
Strabo, 82
Street Light Interference, 140
sublime, 72, 92, 99, 104, 107, 115, 129, 134, 136, 146, 178, 201, 202, 207, 215
Sublime Light, 91, 206
sublime pneuma, 134, 136, 146
Suffering Servant, 60, 49
Sufis, 162
Symeon the New Theologian, 143, 182-184, 191, 196, 201, 202, 204

Symeon the Studite, 182-184, 191

T

Tabor, Mount, 45, 61, 72-75, 88, 115, 126, 139, 175, 179, 182, 191, 192, 201, 204
tachyonic, 206, 207
Talmud, 39, 62
Tantric, 159, 160, 164
Tarsus, 68, 111
Tart, Charles, 95
Telesterion, 81, 84, 85, 89
Tenach, 40, 61
Tenhaeff, W.H.C., 58, 134
Theissen, Gerd, 41
Theosophists, 85, 88, 95
theurgy, 135
Thurston, Herbert, 149
Tibetan Book of the Dead., 87
Tite, S. Michael,
tomb, 38, 63, 65-67, 73, 76, 85, 87, 91, 123, 125, 131, 152, 208
tombstone, 66, 73
Torah, 62
transcendental magic, 135
Transfiguration, 56, 61, 72, 75, 88, 104, 109, 111, 115, 126, 135, 138, 139, 146, 147, 175, 179, 190-193, 197, 200, 201

Tryon, Victor, 31
Tuchman, Barbara, 10

U

UFO, 70, 71, 172
ultra-weak-bioluminescence, 149
Uncreated Light, 189, 191
Upinsky, Arnaud-Aaron, 27, 34

V

Van Haelst, Remi, 147
Vatican, 9, 33
Vehicles of Consciousness, 133
Vergy, Jeanne de, 14, 15, 198, 199
Veronica, 39
Viaud, Prosper, 118
Vignon, Paul, 21, 24
visio dei luminis, 201
Volckringer, J., 147
Vostitzia, 198
VP-8 Image Analyzer, 25

W

Wasson, R. Gordon, 86
Whanger, Alan, 25
Whiteman, J.H.M., 96

Wilhelm, Richard, 107, 108
Wilson, Ian, 17, 18, 20, 21, 33, 198, 214
Witt, R.E., 78
Wojcik, Daniel, 70

Z

Zohar, 77
Zugibe, F.T., 23